Let's Fly Backward

Let's Fly Backward

by
Al Barnes

HORIZON BOOKS　　　　　　　　TRAVERSE CITY, MI

Copyright © 1976 by Al Barnes
and Vicki Barnes
Copyright © 2000 by Horizon Books

Library of Congress Catalog Card Number 75-39182
ISBN 0-915937-07-7 (PB)
ISBN 0-915937-08-5 (HC)

Published by
HORIZON BOOKS, 243 E. Front St., Traverse City, Michigan 49684

DEDICATION

In the year of 1637 Thomas Barnes married Mary (maiden name unknown) and begat three children. Then, as I will explain later, Mary died and Grandfather Barnes married Mary Andrews (Andrus) and sired two children, Thomas and Ebenezer. I am a direct descendent of Ebenezer.

But, I have no intention of dedicating a Handbook of History to Grandfather Thomas.

I wish to pay a tribute to his wife, and to her I dedicate most of this book, a little tribute which she never received in her home near the villages of Farmington and Hartford, in Connecticut.

You see, according to the official records, Mary was arrested after she gave Grandfather Thomas three children, and was charged with harboring (entertaining) evil spirits.

After a period of imprisonment and a "fair" trial, she was found guilty by a jury of her peers and was sentenced to death. The sentence was duly carried out.

The records say that Grandfather Barnes (referred to as Goodman Barnes in the official account) paid the costs of incarceration and execution.

So, Mary Barnes: Let this little book be a sort of monument to you and your memory. I know you weren't a witch. Then, when I think how Grandfather Barnes turned right around and married his housekeeper, Mary Andrews, I feel sort of sad. There must have been some sort of hanky-panky away back there.

Too, I suppose I should dedicate a page or two to my Great Uncle Alfred. He messed around in the city of Chicago and was murdered for his indescretions with the wrong women.

And, I must save a page of dedication for Uncle Luke. He was a veteran of the Civil War. When he departed this vale they had the devil's own time determining who should get his survivor's pension. You see, Uncle Luke had overlooked the matter of divorce from some of his earlier wives. Aunt Mollie finally won out.

There you are Mary Barnes, Uncle Alfred, and Uncle Luke. It's not much at this late date, but it is the very best I can do for you. I think of you often.

Very sincerely yours,
Al

FOREWORD

The trouble with history is that it has a way of looking too dignified. It spells itself with a capital letter and treats all of its subjects the same way; which is to say that it purports to be an important account of the important doings of important people. That is all right, of course, because the whole business undoubtedly is very important indeed, but the trouble is that after a while it tends to lose touch with reality.

For if history is the impressive record of the actions of the important folk—served up, usually, by a historian who comes on the scene as impressively as an old-time English nobleman pulling up to the House of Lords in his private coach-and-four—it rests ultimately on the small events in the unobserved lives of the great majority. The historian may be a notable historian sitting in a library with stacks of manuscripts at his elbows, or a famous journalist perched in the press gallery to watch a great session of the United States Senate; but he can also be a quiet note-taker in rural hamlet or small city, briefly jotting down accounts of the small events that would otherwise go forever unrecorded but that make up all-important sub-stratum to the historical edifice.

Formal history deals with what the leaders and shakers are up to, but it can never be properly understood unless we know about the modest folk who are being led and shaken, and who at times respond to the leading and shaking in quite unexpected ways.

All of which (to get to the point round-about and late, after the manner of the stuffy historian) is what makes books like this one so much worth reading and preserving.

Al Barnes is one of the quiet note-takers.

For many years he has been jotting down the record of what takes place in his own neighborhood. If something happened within reasonable distance of the foot of Grand Traverse Bay, from the day of the first land-looker down to the present, Al Barnes knows about it and has made note of it. He put a great deal of the record together in innumerable newspaper articles, got more of it in between covers in *Vinegar Pie*, and now rounds it off in this book, *Let's Fly Backward*. There is not much here for the headline-hunters, to be sure, but there is much information and solid wisdom put together in such a skillfull, unassuming way that it is remarkably easy and pleasant to read.

Make no mistake about it. The people and events herein described may have been obscure, but they were by no means unimportant. They are the stuff on which formal history is based. To understand the past we must first get it into focus, and Al Barnes does that without even seeming to try. He does not need to try, because he had it in focus right from the start.

When we study history we need facts, of course, but we have an equal need for imagination. Not the imagination that creates supposed facts out of whole cloth, but the imagination that enables us to understand why people did what they did and gave a special shape to the society now occupied by their children. This imagination has to have something to work on; and it is precisely that "something to work on" that you find in books like this one. Reading it, you will have a better understanding of the achievements of this particular part of the state than you would have otherwise.

History is a mosaic made up of innumerable local patterns; an old-fashioned crazy-quilt, perhaps, except that there is more of a pattern there than seems to be right at first. Here is a solid, friendly, unpretentious study of one of those pieces. Those of us who are lucky enough to be a part of the Grand Traverse Bay country owe Al Barnes a debt for bringing it to our attention.

—Bruce Catton

CONTENTS

FOREWORD
INTRODUCTION 13
LET'S FLY BACKWARD 21
  Acme 23
  Bates 27
  Bellaire 30
  Benzonia 33
  Beulah 36
  Buckley 39
  Cedar 42
  Copemish 45
  Elberta 48
  Elk Rapids 51
  Empire 54
  Fife Lake 57
  Frankfort 60
  Glen Arbor 63
  Grawn 66
  Greilickville 69
  Honor 72
  Interlochen 75
  Kalkaska 78
  Kewadin 81
  Kingsley 84
  Lake Ann 87
  Lake Leelanau 90
  Leland 93
  Mancelona 96
  Maple City 99
  Mayfield 102
  Mesick 105

Northport	108
Omena	111
Rapid City	114
South Boardman	117
Summit City	120
Suttons Bay	123
Thompsonville	126
Torch River	129
Traverse City	132
Williamsburg	135
BARNESTORMING THE GRAND TRAVERSE BAY REGION	138
Tour Number One	142
Tour Number Two	151
Tour Number Three	158
Tour Number Four	170
Tour Number Five	177
UNGUIDED TOURS IN THE GRAND TRAVERSE BAY AREA AND ADDITIONAL POINTS OF INTEREST YOU SHOULD VISIT	183
THINGS YOU SHOULD KNOW ABOUT THE GRAND TRAVERSE BAY AREA	185
THE GIRLS	189
RED MEN'S REBUKE	194

INTRODUCTION

This was written by "Mr. History" himself, Jay P. Smith. It was in 1957 while I was working on the book *Vinegar Pie* that I asked him to write something about Traverse City as he remembered it. Always obliging and always an accurate source of historical information and lore, he complied... but too late to be used at that time. Jay is gone but nothing can erase our memory of him. Thank you, Jay.

* * *

Traverse City has always been a fabulous town located in a fabulous community. At the turn of the century it was a lumbering community of approximately six thousand people. There were 14 churches and 21 saloons. Three recognized bordellos and a lot of rough young people ready to keep things on the hum. Sin was in the saddle for both sexes.

It was the town of the fabulous Duff MacDonald, huge bartender who looked a lot like Kaiser Wilhelm; more, and to an embarrassing degree, he looked like the son of the town's founder and only millionaire, Perry Hannah.

It was the town of the legendary Jack Rennie, lumber camp operator, turned town marshall and chief of the city's first fire department. It was the town of a dozen young rake-hells from top families who carried keys to the better saloons for access after closing hours and on Sundays.

Let's start with Duff MacDonald, the huge, splay-footed fellow with great, turned up mustachios, who was drum major of the boy's band. It was Duff who dyed three white chickens green and put them in the window of the Hurry-Back Saloon on St. Patrick's Day.

The Irish were in town from the lumber camps, the saw mills, and the shingle mills of the region and at about ten drinks along the line they grew sentimental about the shamrock colored hens.

Duff finally broke down and admitted he had a few eggs from the green chickens which he planned to use to increase his flock but, if the lads from the "auld sod" really wanted some, they could be purchased for only a dollar a piece. Did they want them? Duff dodged into the back way of Wilhelm and Bartek grocery store, two doors from the Hurry-Back, and bought a dozen eggs for 15c.

Some say he made thirty trips back after more eggs but there was no Internal Revenue Department at that time, so on the number of eggs he passed out at the Hurry-Back no accurate check is available.

Jack Rennie, the chief of the rednecks, enforced the law with his buggy whip; the same one he used in driving his fat, black pacer, Dogwood, hitched to his light, rubber-tired buggy and feuded constantly and in perfectly friendly spirits with the town playboys.

Jack had a system of law enforcement which was all his own and somewhat original. Bums were taken to the city limits, cut sharply across the rump with the lash, and told never to return. They rarely did. Wife beaters felt the sting of the whip as did petty thieves. Jack's whip kept the jail empty and the taxpayers happy.

It was the town to which mill owners from all over the region came for their notorious week-end five card stud poker game at the Park Place Hotel. A player would open for perhaps a carload of number two hardwood and the man of his left might raise him with two car lots of star-A-star shingles. The next man would see the raise and up it a section of hardwood, mostly maple, near a siding in Garfield township.

Oldsters still tell solemnly about what a good dancer Frank Kratochvil was. He ran a brewery with a tap room in connection and could dance a full set with a full beer balanced on his head and never spill a drop.

It was the town where old man Whinnery, who usually braided his long red beard for Sunday, ran an oyster house in a little hole in the wall. One morning he was found dead on the floor of his place of business. A crowd quickly gathered outside and, of course, someone said, "What is the matter?" Dan Round, a short wag who couldn't see very well over the heads of the taller competitors, murmured the frightening word "smallpox." In less than a minute there was nobody left to help old Doc Ashton get the body to Anderson's undertaking parlor. No one, that is, except Dan.

Only in Traverse City could a drug clerk spill a few drops of croton oil in the cider at a church social, thereby putting that sect on a two day diet of toast and tea, and at the same time get away with it.

It was in Traverse City that Jim Keho, ticket agent for the old C. and W.M., mentioned to Dave Campbell and Tracy Gillis up at the Elks that he left the baggage room door unlocked and there were two cans of maple syrup there for Chief Rennie. Dave and Tracy were two of the lads who feuded with the chief. An hour later, in Tracy's cutter, they were driving to the Rennie home with the two cans emptied of maple syrup and filled with machine oil. When they delivered it to Mrs. Rennie, the chief being on duty, she asked who it was from and they told her Fred Hunter, Front Street clothier. Jack took one taste of machine oil on his flapjacks the next morning, sputtered, chuckled, hitched up Dogwood and in almost no time at all had a surprised Fred Hunter in a Front Street snowbank, washing his face. He could go along with the gag.

It was a town in which three printers who worked Saturday night and drank at their work, caught three live rats in a trap. When they went to the Hotel Whiting for breakfast they took the rats with them but manager Compton ordered them out. Hurt and disillusioned, they moved on to Ole Bostrums Saloon, still toting the rats for which they could find no suitable home.

By this time they were sentimental about the little captives and wanted to place them well. The Congregational church bell, a short distance away sounded, calling the faithful to worship and at the same time lighting a gleam in the eyes of the printers. Without a word, they stood up, had two quick drinks and went to the Congregational church. What better atmosphere in which to leave three homeless rats. So they turned them loose just inside the church door and went happily back to Ole's place.

The town lushs, and they were myriad, never failed to observe the social amenities. When invited to a whist party, they might fall flat on their faces when the hostess opened the door, but everyone of them had tempered their breath with sen-sen or orange peel.

The company store featured white china cuspidors with a wreath of blue forget-me-nots around the outside for the Christmas trade. Pa was just as delighted to find one of these under the Christmas tree as he would be today with a new deep freeze.

Traverse City was always a great Town for theater. I recall one time I was promised a ticket to Uncle Tom's Cabin show if I would lead the bloodhound in the street parade at noon. Front Street was called the Cedar Swamp because it had telephone, electric lights, and telegraph poles studded thickly along the board sidewalk. In a red tunic that came to my knees and cap that sat down over my ears, I led the parade with a friendly old mastiff, which twice each day during the performance, once at the matinee and once in the evening, had to chase Eliza across the ice in Steinbergs Grand Opera House. During the parade, I found that the mastiff was a lot stronger than I, and to him those telephone poles were a new found paradise. Never had a parade, nor even a funeral procession, moved so slowly down Front Street and I was embarrassed. I was so embarrassed I never even asked for my ticket.

A demure grass widow came to town one day and opened a dress making shop over the city drug store. She was a shy little thing but pretty as the dickens. Three weeks later a physician walked into the State Bank and asked for a loan of a thousand dollars. "All right, doctor," the cashier said, "what denominations does the dressmaker want?" The medico flushed and flared; "Oh don't get excited," the cashier said, "you're the third man who has been in here this evening after a thousand dollars just to keep her mouth shut." The next day the dressmaker had moved to new blackmail fields.

This was the town of Traverse City where a very prominent citizen maintained a room on South Union

Street in which he established a female member of nearly every stock company which played a week's stand at Steinbergs or the City Opera House. One budding actress, so maintained for a week, refused to leave when the troupe moved on to Manistee. The next week the local weekly carried a little box on the front page which said and we quote: "There are only three white elephants in captivity and, (naming the man,) has one of them." The next day the man with a weakness for actresses purchased the weekly.

This is the town where Mode Rich and Charlie Hallberg ran a saloon. Every night they divided the money in the till and when the bills came due they each forked up half of it.

Lumberjacks, coming in from the camps with a winter's paycheck first bought some new stag pants, a new felt hat, a checkered shirt, visited the barber shop, and then went out to George Robinson's or the Swamp House for a fling with the girls. The money they had left they gave to Mode or Charlie and then started their serious drinking. After three or four rush days, Mode or Charlie handed them a pint of whiskey and they knew they had drunk up all their credit and they would shoulder their turkeys and hit the road back to camp. We never once heard the bookkeeping of Mode and Charlie questioned.

This was a town that always had a bang-up Fourth of July celebration with a special rate excursions for all the towns around and oddly enough these affairs were largely financed by saloon keepers, who, the law said very specifically, must be closed by ten o'clock each night and all day Sunday, as well as on legal holidays.

Quite a few of the old printers picked up extra money by tending bar Sunday and holidays. The fun was rough in those days but tinged with consideration.

One morning following Halloween night, the community boasted that only six privies were left standing and all six belonged to widow ladies.

This was the town where the local paper chronicled that the Perry boys had spent the day fishing up the Boardman river and returned with 400 brook trout. A week later the same paper announced that Will Hobbs and Chuck Parker had been over to "Dam One" on the Manistee river fishing for grayling and they only brought home 125 but they intended to go back when the fishing was better.

Now the Christians have taken the upper hand and Traverse City is almost a model community. Once in a while you can find a pine plank and it may still show the pock marks made by the caulks of the drivers' boots.

LET'S FLY BACKWARD

This historical guide to some of the villages, towns and cities of the Grand Traverse area surrounding its capitol, Traverse City, was written over a 15-year period. Started in 1961, it grew slowly as time to work permitted.

For that reason, it was impossible to keep pace with the changes and growth of the many towns and villages. Aerial photographs taken today could well be outdated tomorrow.

For that reason, some of the photos will show change within the memory of the reader. Many of the photos were re-taken, but in some instances it was difficult or unrealistic. If your new home doesn't show, please forgive us.

As an example is the photo of the city of Traverse City and its waterfront. The Morgan-McCool buildings are shown still standing. And it is better so. Just as Perry Hannah was a monumental influence in the beginnings of Traverse City, so were the Morgans in the development and growth of the cherry industry. We are glad we can use the photo as we "Fly Backward."

—Al Barnes

ACME
ONCE CALLED "WHITEWATER"

The village of Acme, located on the east arm of Grand Traverse Bay, about seven miles north of Traverse City, was once heralded as a coming industrial town. The folks who were promoting the fledgling community talked "big city" language.

The beginning of the village was when a farmer named L.S. Hoxsie arrived from Lenawee County and purchased a tract of land where the central part of the town now stands. The first town meeting of Whitewater Township was held in the Hoxsie home.

Hoxsie laid out the village and sold a number of lots for homesites. From that time on, there was a bustle of activity in Acme.

In 1858, Hoxsie built a sawmill on the creek, later selling it to his son, John.

John Hoxsie added to the family holdings by building a woolen mill in what is now the heart of the present town. A man named Scripture was financially interested in the woolen mill and, for many years it prospered despite competition by the Buller Woolen Mill which was built a short distance upstream.

23

Woolen blankets, manufactured by the Scripture and Hoxsie Mill, were sold to the Asylum in Traverse City and, until a few years ago, some of the blankets were still in storage in the institution.

There was also a shingle mill in operation in the village and there was a belief that Acme, served by rails, would be a large community.

To more accurately picture the industrial setting of the village, the Buller Woolen Mill was located northeast of the Masonic building and the Scripture and Hoxsie Mill was southwest of the present post office.

Between the years of 1880 and 1890, the village was booming. There was a hotel located at the northeast intersection of the highways and there were several stores doing business.

The Acme post office served other mail stations of the area including Yuba, Bates, Mable, and Angell.

But it was inevitable that the woolen mills could not meet the competition of the mills in the metropolitan areas where wages were near slavery and merchandise cheaper. One of the mills moved to Traverse City in an effort to reorganize but barely opened its doors before it folded. The other mill died where it was born.

Then a greater blow befell the community. The timber which was the lifeblood of the mills grew scarce and the mills were forced to close. The cedar which supplied the shingle mill disappeared and that, too, closed.

For a time the village of Acme remained static insofar as growth was concerned. The old hotel was razed and the stores closed one by one.

But Acme had an advantage. It was located on the popular Grand Traverse Bay and it was only a matter of time before summer homes and resort property gave new life and prospects to the area.

The post office, closed at the end of the lumbering era, has been re-established. New business has been attracted and, once again, the village of Acme is alive and well. It is a delightful community to visit . . . one with a fascinating background in history.

BATES
NAMED FOR A FAMILY

The birth of the village of Bates was not an event to ring the bells of the nation.

First public announcement that such a town existed was a brief note in the *Grand Traverse Herald*, published in Traverse City. On page six of the *Herald* there was this brief mention:

"By the way, the postoffice named Bates was opened to the public on Thursday, January 21, 1892."

This date, however, disagrees with the records of the postal department which indicate that the postoffice was opened on September 21, 1891.

The first postmaster was Lyman P. Fox and the tiny village was named for the pioneer Bates family of Traverse City.

There are no records at the Grand Traverse county courthouse that would indicate that there was ever a recorded plat of the village.

Bates is located in Acme township on Highway 72 and, for a time after its birth, there was some indication that it would be a community of great promise.

There was a booming business for Chicago and West Michigan Railroad in the shipping of cordwood, lumber, logs, finished lumber, tanbark, and, lastly, thousands of bushels of potatoes.

Shortly after the opening of the postoffice, a "mail-catcher" was installed to faciliate the pick-up of mail at the station. The residents of the community began, about this time, a campaign for a "flag-station" and this was innaugurated in March, 1892. On March 29 of that year, 13 passengers boarded the southbound train.

In April, 1892, Postmaster Fox was named ticket agent at the depot and he reported that the sum of $54.00 was taken in for rates during a two week period.

Social life in the village was that of any other town still in swaddling clothes. The young folks had parties and played "Snap and catch 'em" and "Charlie, catch the squirrel."

The general store, located west of the rails, did a booming business and the potato became king. A large potato warehouse was erected and thousands of bushels of produce were shipped.

But Bates had no sound industry to rely on when the timber was gone. Too, it was located too near the villages of Acme and Williamsburg.

In 1931, a fatal blow was struck when the postoffice was closed. Mary Knopf was postmistress at the time.

Today, where Bates stood, there is only a pleasant little cluster of homes. It is still prime farming area and the rails occasionally see a creeping train. The depot has been razed and the store has long since closed and been torn down.

It is a lovely drive for visiting friends and a bright memory for those who knew it in its brighter and more bustling days.

BELLAIRE
BUILT ON HISTORIC INDIAN MOUNDS

The village of Bellaire, Antrim County, has a background of history more fascinating than the mere fact that it is a pioneer community which weathered depressions, the wane of the timber, and political difficulties.

A portion of the village is built on old mounds (presumably Indian burial) and, over a period of years, scores of artifacts have been uncovered.

The village was first platted in 1878 when the state supreme court ruled that the removal of the county seat from Elk Rapids would be legal.

The village plat has been expanded since that early day until it now occupies both sides of Intermediate river in the Chain-of-Lakes.

The first postoffice was established in July, 1881, and it was recorded as at the village of Keno. Later, because of the purity of the air and the pleasant climate, the name was changed to Bellaire. The first postmaster was Rufus Hall.

Excellent water power at the site of the village gave

impetus to industry and to the establishment of an electric power company.

Too, the village was located in the heart of thousands of acres of excellent hardwood. This gave rise to the manufacture of such items as rolling pins, butter dishes, wooden scoops, wooden pitchers, and similar hardwood products.

The village was incorporated in 1891. First officers to serve the new town were F.W. Bechtold, president; Fred Zoon, clerk; Alfred A. Hickox, assessor; and J.C. Abbot, treasurer.

The location of the village in the Chain-of-Lakes area makes it an ideal vactionland. Summer guests number into the thousands and the popularity of the community continues to grow.

It is one of the really beautiful villages of the north, having excellent public services combined with an aggressive and forward citizenry.

BENZONIA
FOUNDED BY A CHRISTIAN SCHOOL

The village of Benzonia came into being as the direct result of the Christian zeal of a small group of pioneers. Rev. Charles Bailey, John Bailey, who was his brother, and their brothers-in-law, Rev. W.M. Fairfield and Rev. Amzi Barber, wished to build a mission settlement where temperance and anti-slavery would be dominant.

Their choice, after long journeys and much study, was in the Crystal Lake area, now Benzie county. That was in 1858 and Bailey and his family were the first settlers.

Only five years after the arrival of the Bailey family, an educational institution of ambitious proportions was built and Grand Traverse College was given birth. Church (Congregational) and college worked hand in hand for the betterment of the community, and the pioneer settlement prospered. The entire settlement was built around the ambition and untiring labor of Bailey. He operated the first general store and

established a coach and mail line between Traverse City and Frankfort.

In 1880, Rev. Bailey and his family left the Benzonia community. With his departure, the affairs of the settlement and the college fell into other and equally capable hands.

But it was not destined that Benzonia should be a college town. As time rolled on, the college closed its doors. It was the question of whether an institution, supported by contributions alone, could exist in competition with tax supported schools.

The college, after a final reorganization as Benzonia Academy, closed in 1918.

Although the village was built for and around the church and college, it was so firmly built by those pioneer settlers, that it continued to live.

Not destined to become a ghost town and monument in memory, Benzonia continues to be a beautiful and active village.

Summer homes and year round homes are hidden behind lush groves. On every hand there is a magnificent view from the glacial hills. It is, indeed a beautiful and progressive town.

BEULAH
ONCE BEULAH VIEW RESORT

On the southeast shore of sparkling Crystal Lake is located one of the most charming villages in northern Michigan. It was known to many people of another era as Beulah View Resort.

Beulah came into being on December 9, 1890, at 2:00 p.m. when the original plat was recorded at the Benzie County courthouse. The plat was sponsored by Charles E. Bailey and Lorinda Bailey and the influence of the church by which Bailey was inspired was reflected in the name of one of the streets, "Beulah Land Drive."

Prior to the platting of the village, the water level of Crystal Lake had been lowered through an attempt to cut an outlet to Lake Michigan and establish lake traffic. An error in survey caused the lake to drop several feet, creating a beautiful beach around its entire circumference. Where the main business section of the

village now stands there was once a lush growth of cattails and swamp grass.

Streets running parallel to Crystal Lake were named Lake street, Center street and Benzie boulevard. Running at right angles to the lake, the streets were originally named First street, which continued into the south part of the village at East street, Second street, Third street, and Court street. Other streets which criss-crossed the sprawling village were Lake View drive, Crystal avenue, Commercial avenue, Clark street, and Pleasant street.

A second addition to the village was dedicated on September 23, 1900, when Lucy Merritt, William Phelps and his wife, Nancy; and William Wenegar and his wife, Maggie, presented a survey for record.

Cold Creek was then known as Crystal Inlet, and had two branches, Eden branch and Cold Spring Creek.

As property owners in the Beulah area began to realize the potential of the village and the surrounding community as a resort and vacation area, new additions were recorded. There were Shore Acres, Sears Addition, and others.

Beulah, still Crystal City and Beulah View Resort, insofar as records go, is indeed a beautiful community.

This photo was made when celery was king in the village and shows, in the foreground, the well known Trapp celery gardens.

BUCKLEY TRIED TO STAY "DRY"

In 1905, Glen and Kate Brigham conceived the idea of platting a village in the very north part of Wexford county on what is now highway M-37. The plat, for some unknown reason, was redone that same year and the name of Buckley and Douglas Lumber Company appears on the plat with that of Mr. and Mrs. Bringham. Old timers assume that the original plat offered "too much land to a lot" and the village would be scattered all over the north end of the county.

Only two highway-miles from the village of Wexford, the settlement was called New Wexford. Later, due to the great influence of the Buckley and Douglas Lumber Company, the name was changed to Buckley, after Edward Buckley.

It was incorporated in 1907 and, at the peak of its prosperity had a population of over a thousand people. Present population is just under 300, up somewhat during the past few years.

Buckley had a problem in law enforcement in those early days. The poeple of the community voted the village "dry" but it was a problem to keep it that way. The North Star Saloon, a thriving business in the village, was forced to move when the law went into effect. The move was only about half a mile, across the line into Grand Traverse county, where it continued to furnish spirits to the residents of the young village and headaches to the law enforcement officers.

Wexford, on a steep decline because of the lack of rail facilities and the public interest in Buckley, continued to lose popularity. Many of the residents of Wexford moved to the new town and many more moved away.

With the wane of the timber, the village still lived. Good roads make it a pleasant place in which to live and the quiet, rural atmosphere was attractive to many older people.

A recent survey of the residents of the village showed that 46% of the families in the community have lived there from 25 to 50 years and 14% have lived there more that 50 years.

CEDAR
STAVES, HOOPS, SHINGLES, LUMBER

With a preponderance of fine cedar timber in the Centerville area of Leelanau county, it was only natural that mills should be erected for the manufacture of lumber and shingles. With the coming of the Sullivan Lumber Company, the little community was known as Cedar City.

In 1892, the Manistee and Northeastern Railway gave the town new vigor and growth. A stave and hoop mill was erected and the population was variously estimated at over 500 people. The census prior to 1900 listed Cedar as having 681 residents. One oldtimer said, "They took the figure from a hat because Cedar wasn't that big."

In the years when timber began to wane, Sullivan bought the Dewey Stave Mill and used it to manufacture hardwood lumber.

Charlie Billman built the first general store in Cedar

in 1886 and, in early 1900, organized a bank which operated for a quarter of a century.

Farm land around the village is exceptionally productive and lured hundreds of settlers of Polish heritage. Today the town is sometimes referred to as "Little Poland." But these people have been the backbone of the community economy.

The main street of the village looks, today, much as it did half a century ago. The business places change on occasion. An old one closes and a new one opens... but in almost every instance, the names of the owners or operators reflect the Polish family background.

Cedar creek, which flows through the north part of Cedar, has been a fisherman's favorite for a century. In addition, today, a boat can navigate the stream from its mouth on the south end of Lake Leelanau to the heart of the village.

The old railroad tracks are gone these many years. Where the depot stood, there is a pleasant park and mooring for visiting watercraft.

All-in-all, Cedar didn't give up and die. It and its people just rolled with the punches of progress and kept on being a nice village with a lot of nice people.

COPEMISH
NAMED FOR A TREE

In the northwestern corner of Cleon township, Manistee county, there is a tiny village with the drive to live. Established in 1886, Copemish took its name from the Indian word meaning "tree with the smooth bark" or "big beech." The word was originally spelled kop-i-mish and the first white settlers in the area accepted the name for their village.

Where the Indians held council meetings under the spreading branches of the giant beech tree, the Copemish council now holds its modern council meetings to guide the prosperity of the community.

The first merchantile building was a company store owned by the Buckley and Douglas Lumbering Firm. The post office was housed in the general store.

The village was located in the very heart of a fabulous stand of hardwood and it was only natural that there should be flooring mills, and a wooden dish mill which made butterbowls, rolling pins, and similar

wooden ware. There was a harness manufacturing firm and several other business places, all doing a bustling business. This, however, was before the seemingly inexhaustable supply of hardwood trees was depleted.

With the removal of the timber, business gradually went into a decline. The sawmills closed for want of raw material.

The coming of the Toledo and Ann Arbor railroad in 1889 gave brief new life to the village and an assurance that it would not become a ghost town.

Incorporated in 1891, Copemish took precautions to maintain sufficient community spirit to insure its future. Agriculture of a specialized nature was encouraged, and millions of gladioli bulbs have been grown and shipped to market. There is a mushrooming industry in the growing of top quality strawberries and, each July, the village celebrates a Strawberry Festival to publicize the fruit.

ELBERTA
IN MEMORY OF A PEACH

Frankfort City was platted in 1866 and the plat was recorded on St. Valentine's Day, 1867. It was located on the opposite shore of the large harbor across from the then new village of Frankfort.

The actual survey of the plat was made by a Traverse City man, George Steele, on authority from George M. Cartwright and was first known as South Town.

It was in 1870 that the Frankfort Iron Furnace Company opened a $200,000.00 plant. It was believed that, with the advantage of ample harbor facilities, the industry would be the backbone of the future and an incentive for additional industry to locate there.

The plant, in the words of the pioneers, "was ahead of its time," and was abandoned after a few years of operation.

In 1894, South Frankfort was incorporated as a village. The timber was becoming less and less

important as a sustaining item in the economy of the community and, as the land was cleared, it was discovered that fruit did well on the light soil.

Peaches were planted extensively and one variety, the Elberta, showed an affinity for both the climate and the soil. So promising did the fruit industry look that, in 1911, a bill was passed in the legislature changing the name of the village from Frankfort City to Elberta.

The Ann Arbor railroad, establishing a water terminus at the village, gave indication that there would, some day, be a city of considerable proportions on the south shore of Lake Aux Becs Scies, later called Betsie Lake.

More than 99% of the shipping tonnage in and out of Benzie county originates or terminates in the village of Elberta and, despite the proximity of its sister village of Frankfort, all major docking facilities are in Elberta. In fact, the entire south half of the harbor water lies within that village.

Today Elberta is still the terminus of the rails for the Ann Arbor.

ELK RAPIDS
IT STARTED BIG

There was a day when the village of Stevens bid fair to become a city long before its neighbor, Traverse City, could get its sawdust-coated feet on solid ground.

Stevens, later to be named Elk Rapids by official postal designation, was platted in 1852 by A. S. Wadsworth.

From the very beginning it showed rapid growth. In 1853 a school was established and in that same year, the post office was approved.

In 1855 Henry M. Noble arrived in the village as an employee of M. Craw and Company. In 1856 the firm was dissolved and Wirt Dexter and Henry Noble established the beginnings of a giant in business and industry: Dexter and Noble.

The money panic of 1857 was felt by the village but the Dexter and Noble firm continued to grow. It was the financial backbone of the community and, at one

time, their merchantile stock was larger than that of Marshall Field in Chicago.

In 1864 the village had a population of 300 people and Elk Rapids was the county seat.

The *Traverse Bay Eagle* was first published in Elk Rapids and was the forerunner of the *Traverse City Record Eagle.*

Elk Rapids continued to grow. With the establishment of an iron smelter, charcoal kilns, wood alcohol distillery, a large cement plant, and other industry, Elk Rapids, had tremendous impact on the pioneer growth of the Grand Traverse region.

In 1872 the *Elk Rapids Progress,* a weekly newspaper, was established and is still being published.

Flour mills, shingle mills, lath mills, miscellaneous industry—all continued to add to the prosperity of the village.

The lumber business, then the lifeblood of the village, died. Dexter and Noble, as well as other lumbermen, were forced to go farther and farther inland for raw material. The economy of the iron smelter faltered because of the retreating timberline and the difficulty of transportation.

The gigantic cement plant closed and Elk Rapids settled back to enjoy a placid and prosperous transition. It is now a quiet community which is favored by nature as a vacation land. New industry, not on the grand scale of the timber business, has moved in, and the popularity of the village still continues to grow.

EMPIRE
THE VILLAGE IN THE DUNES

The village of Empire had its true beginning when John Larue, one of the "three Johns" of Leelanau county, cleared a small piece of land in 1851 and brought his family to the region to live.

The brisk lumber business which favored the village caused healthy growth and, as the timber business neared its end, there was great activity in fruit culture.

So important did the future of the fruit industry seem that one of the pioneer lumbering firms, hoping to make a transition from timber into fruit culture, planted hundreds of acres of orchards, many of which are still standing and producing.

The Empire Lumber Company, T. Wilcie Company, Potter and Struthers, and many more firms led a march forward in the building of the village.

Beginning with only a farm home, isolated in the wilderness, Empire developed into a centrally important manufacturing town and lumber shipping center.

A large dock accommodated shipping interests, and the rails distributed inland and connected the village with other areas.

Later there was every indication that Empire would become a banking center for the northern part of the state. A sound banking firm (Empire Exchange) was established and flourished. The village still boasts a traditionally fine banking record.

While the first settler arrived in the area in 1851, it was not until October, 1895, that the board of supervisors met to consider the matter of Empire as a recognized village.

First officers of the new village were E. R. Dailey, manager of the Empire Lumber Company, president; Fritz Rohr, clerk; Dr. S. A. Gates, treasurer; William Sullivan, assessor; and Michael F. Horen was the first village marshal.

Empire never retreated, nor did it stand still. It remains a rural village but an unusually progressive one. It is a part of the Grand Traverse Region which reflects progressive thinking by its residents. It enjoys an extremely prosperous resort and vacation business, encouraged by the cool breezes of Lake Michigan and the pleasantness of its people.

FIFE LAKE
ONCE TWO VILLAGES

The village of Fyfe Lake (later Fife Lake) came into existence on a June day, 1872, when J.L. Shaw and a group of associates from Grand Rapids platted the village. At about the same time, T.T. Bates, a Traverse City newspaperman, platted another section of the town and the two communties were known, for years, as North Fife Lake and South Fife Lake.

Originally the railway, The Grand Rapids and Indiana, pushing northward into the beautiful and verdant pine forest, made an error in naming the village. William Fife, Acme, Michigan, a highway official, was one of the original surveyors in the area. In fact, the lake was named in his honor. The railroad officials simply mis-spelled the name, "Fyfe" instead of "Fife."

For years there was considerable personal strife between factions in North Fife Lake and South Fife Lake. No one ever accused a resident directly, but the

depot, a target of strife, located in North Fife Lake, burned without evident cause. It was later rebuilt in South Fife Lake.

The first mill in the village was that of Tracy and Thurber. It made an initial cut in August, 1872. It is incidental that the first log produced 600 feet of first quality pine lumber.

In June, 1872, J.B. Lancaster opened a small store, and business was excellent. He later enlarged and modernized and was one of the more prosperous pioneer businessmen of the town.

Rivalry between "Uppertown" and "Lowertown," as the two segments were often called, was sharp. The first postmaster in the north section was James Montieth and the office was soon thereafter moved to the lower part of the village.

Located just off U.S. 131, Fife Lake is one of the popular resort settlements in the area.

FRANKFORT
HARBOR OF GIANTS

Before the present century, the prediction was made that the harbor at the vilalge on the Betsie river would, one day, be able to berth the largest ships afloat on the Great Lakes. The prediction came true and Betsie river, subsequently named Frankfort, has one of the finest harbors on Lake Michigan.

Frankfort had its beginnings in 1859 when H.R. Sanger laid out a plat of 16 blocks. This was subsequently set aside when a group of organized persons platted the beginnings of the present village.

The first building lot in the new village was purchased by William H. Coggshall, who built the first home and served as postmaster for several years.

First attempts by a land company to construct dock facilities were handicapped by bad weather and no real progress toward a major harbor improvement was made until 1866 when the government gave assistance with a grant of $98,000.00.

First large work program on the harbor was started in 1867 when Hubbell and Whitewood arrived with their dredging equipment to deepen the channel and construct facilities.

From that date the village gave signs of healthy growth. Victor Satterlee built the first hotel and boarding house (Frankfort House) in 1867, and J.B. Delbridge constructed the Delbridge House, later to be known as Park House.

The first doctor to serve the Frankfort community was Dr. T. Harvey who arrived in 1867, having previously been in practice in Detroit.

One of the pioneer businessmen and one who served in many capacities in the village was John B. Collins who operated a drug store and was postmaster for many years.

Frankfort is, today, a beautiful village which reflects the careful planning of the pioneers. It is the heart of a thriving vacation business and the home of hundreds of wonderful people, many of whom are descendants of the pioneers.

GLEN ARBOR
LITTLE BUT LOVELY

From a half mile in the air, looking down where the pleasant village of Glen Arbor is located, it is difficult to see the bustling activity that is hidden by the heavily wooded terrain.

Yet Glen Arbor, a tiny village which was first settled in 1854, is the hub of business and social activity in the little Leelanau county community.

A great amount of the history of the community lies buried in the tiny cemetery near the village. Overgrown and wooded, the cemetery is the last resting place of the pioneers who helped found the settlement.

First arrivals at the village site were "four Johns": John LaRue, John Fisher, John Dorsey, and John Helm, and the first steamer to put in at the tiny harbor on Lake Michigan was the *Saginaw*. The *Saginaw* anchored off shore to unload a sawmill which George Ray subsequently operated to cut much of the lumber that went into the building of the village.

Originally, the village was located on the shore of the lake. Cold winter winds out of the north made it logical to move the site inland a short distance where it is now located.

George Ray, owner of the first sawmill, was also the first school teacher and postmaster.

One of the key figures in the later development of the Glen Arbor community was Dr. William H. Walker. He arrived early, possibly at the same time the "four Johns" arrived, and set about developing a cranberry business near the present village. It became a considerable industry and prospered for many years.

The village today is as modern as any in the middle west. The giant stand of timber is no longer on the landscape and the lumberjacks with their caulked boots no longer visit the eating places. The violin and "mouthorgan" no longer scream their square dance tunes and the village has taken on an aura of quiet beauty.

It is one of the most popular vacation spots in Michigan and, in and around Glen Arbor, live a new generation... friendly people who still invite you in for a cup of coffee and ask you to "set a spell."

GRAWN
BUILT IN THREE CORNERS

The village of Blackwood, later Grawn Station, and still later Grawn, after a pioneer family, is a tri-cornered village in Blair Township, Grand Traverse county. It is one of the smallest platted villages in northern Michigan.

Blackwood was named for Jesse R. Blackwood who owned a majority of the lots in the original plat. The survey of the village was entered and approved May 13, 1891.

The original owners of village lots, in addition to those owned by Blackwood, were Mr. and Mrs. William Gibbs, Mr. and Mrs. Joseph Schmith, Mr. and Mrs. Charles McIntose, Mr. and Mrs. Harrison Harr, and Mr. and Mrs. Charles Hess.

An oddity in the orignal plat filing was the fact that Mrs. Joseph Schmith, "Emma," could not write her name and her cross was made and witnessed.

There were few streets in the village. Running north

and south there was Wilcox street, then, to the east was Ewing, and the other north-south street was State street.

Brook street was the only east-west street recorded. The location of the plat, between the Chicago and Western Michigan railroad and the intersection of the Northport-Newaygo state road, made it one of the smallest pioneer villages.

Despite the small size of the town, it was prosperous and bustling. There was the Hotel Pound at the corners of Brook and State streets. There was a large general store, and just south of the general store was the blacksmith shop, one of the really large ones in the region.

On lot 26, State street, was the little telephone exchange. A large potato and grain warehouse occupied lots 6 and 7 on Brook street.

In addition to the several routine business places in the village, there was a number of lesser institutions and Grawn was popular across the north part of the state.

While the village was confined within the triangle, there were two minor additions to the plat. There was the Fouts addition which was cut from the property of Sarah Fouts, and a smaller one taken from the B.E. Crandall property. This ended the growth of the village of Grawn.

GREILICKVILLE
SUBURBAN VILLAGE

On the west shore, at the head of the west arm of Grand Traverse bay, lies a pleasant and growing village. In reality it is difficult to point to a dividing line between the progressive village and the city of Traverse City.

In its beginning it was named for one of the early pioneer families, and a postoffice was assigned under the name of Norrisville. The postoffice was located on the shore of the bay just east of Cherry Bend road.

A gristmill was operated for nearly a half century and was located on Cedar creek. Gordon Pharo later remodeled the old gristmill into a modern home.

The name was changed to Greilickville when the Norris family moved to other parts and the Greilick family erected a large mill on the bay shore.

Before the turn of the century, there was a scattering of small homes overlapping the line between Traverse City and Greilickville. This "barrier" of

residential places was dubbed "Slabtown" because of the type of construction utilized.

Greilickville, like all other lumbering communities, experienced a loss of population as the timber was removed. The postoffice was discontinued and the village became a part of Traverse City insofar as identity was concerned.

Politically a part of Leelanau county, recent years have seen a sudden surge of growth. In addition to scores of new homes, not only along the shores of Cedar Lake, but throughout the village area, there has been a healthy business growth.

Never an incorporated village, the area people have, at various times, considered this possibility.

HONOR HAD FOREIGN INDUSTRY

While the village of Honor actually owes its beginning to a foreign industry, the first plat was surveyed and recorded by Robert Buchan and his wife, Martha, on July 22, 1895. The plat was presented to William Jay, Register of Deeds, at 4:00 p.m. on that date and was called Buchan's addition to the village of Honor. It embraced 69 lots and was the nucleus of the present village.

However, the little town in the wilderness, somewhat off the beaten path and not widely known, was given a firm grip on life on August 24, 1895, when the Guelph Patent Company, Limited, London, England, filed a plat of 102 lots and opened a large manufacturing plant in the village.

The company, after considerable survey, found that the supply of hardwood in the area was seemingly unlimited for the manufacture of hardwood beverage casks. The casks were about the size of the present day "pony" and were exceptionally heavy.

Streets in the new village were called Platte, Main, Mill, Henry, and Cedar.

The Guelph Patent Cask Company did a bustling business for some time, but the construction of railroads into the community, the Manistee and West Michigan, the State Lumber Company railroad, and one owned by T. Wilce, Empire, all began drawing timber from the area and the cask manufacturers found themselves with a factory and no hardwood.

There were, however, additions to the village within the present century. As late as 1908, a plat, recorded by John C. VanBlaircome and his wife, Harriet, had only nine lots. Then, on August 20, 1909, another plat was recorded. It was owned by John Scheuburn, and his wife, Blanche; Fred C. Kucks, and his wife, Oliefie; and Mary Ann Marcham.

Honor was not advertised as a resort town in the early days, nor was it an agricultural center. Roads were built and access was made easy, permitting the fine fishing streams and lakes of the community to become better known.

Word of the friendly community spread rapidly and, today, Honor is one of the family of friendly, progressive communities which make up the Grand Traverse Region.

INTERLOCHEN
KNOWN ACROSS THE NATION

It is difficult to understand why a village, as modernly platted and planned as Interlochen would have failed to reach metropolis status.

In 1890 Edwin E. Benedict, his wife, Sophia, Alexander Lamberg and his wife, Katherine, dedicated the plat of the village of Interlochen.

The streets running east and west were numbered from First street to Eleventh street. The public right of way areas running north and south were designated as avenues. The names of the north-south streets were East avenue, Grand avenue, Mechanics avenue, Commercial avenue, East Railroad and West Railroad avenues, Fashion Avenue, Artist avenue, and West avenue.

The village was platted at the junction of the Michigan and North Western railroad. The Manistee and Northeastern rails were abandoned and removed when the pine and hardwood was depleted.

Interlochen, at the peak of its existence, was a bustling town. With the timber business, two rails to serve the community, excellent recreational qualifications, it had everything in its favor for a prosperous future. The small village of Wylie, mainly the station of the Wylie Cooperage Plant, operated only a stone throw to the southwest. That, too, with the end of the lumbering activities, died.

Actually, Interlochen never really ceased to live. It is still a beautiful village. Although the old streets are overgrown with sod and trees, the main highway is still a beaten path for countless thousands of summer guests as well as the permanent residents of the town.

The National Music Camp, world renowned, and Interlochen Arts Academy, are almost within the village limits and attract the talented youth of the nation.

A modern and progressive school has replaced the old rural school house. The old false front buildings are gone and in their stead are modern business places... few but firm.

KALKASKA
TRULY AN OASIS

In the very center of the plains area of the Grand Traverse Region lies the pleasant and industrious village of Kalkaska. In all directions stretch the seemingly endless, level, cut-over area, once covered by a heavy stand of pine and hardwood.

The village takes its name from the county of which it is the "capital." In the first place, the county was named from an Indian chieftain, Wabassee. It was later named Kalcaska and subsequently the name was changed to Kalkaska.

In 1872, A.A. Abbott, Decatur, Michigan, constructed a mill at the present site of the village of Kalkaska. His mill was on the north branch of the Boardman River and his purchase of 1,000 acres of timbered land gave him ample raw material with which to work.

The following year the community took on the look

of a village as settlers began to arrive and erect log homes.

In 1873 the Congregational church was established and, in 1887, Kalkaska was incorporated as a village.

The village, despite its early isolation, supported a promising newspaper. The *Kalkaskian* was published in 1874 and, in 1911, the *Kalkaska Leader* was established. Later these two publications merged under the management of N. J. Tinklepaugh and the merger still lives, although ownership has changed.

A tragic blow was struck in 1877 (January 23) when fire destroyed several business places in the village. Before it could be brought under control, the Clayton House was destroyed as was the R.S. Abbott store, M.D. Mapes general store, and the business of Coakley and Moore. In 1908 fire again destroyed a part of the main street.

The first school in the village was organized in 1873. Lizzie Farnham was the first teacher and received eight dollars a week for a term of eight weeks beginning in June. A private dwelling was rented for a school house at a cost of one dollar a week.

In 1874 a sum of $100 was appropriated to construct a new school which was finished and ready for use at the opening of school in November.

Kalkaska weathered the wane of timber. It is located in the heart of excellent fishing territory and has a splendid resort business. Of more recent times, oil has been found deep beneath the surface and a new prosperity has come to the village.

The National Trout Festival, an annual spring event, brings thousands of sportsmen to the bustling resort community.

KEWADIN
NAMED FOR A CHIETAIN

Kewadin is a historically important spot on the map. It is the center of an outstanding resort area and has one of the most romantic name-histories of any town in the Grand Traverse area.

In the year of 1884 the following postoffices were active in Antrim county: Alba, Atwood, Bellaire, Central Lake, Chestonia, Clam Lake, Creswell, Eastport, Echo, Elk Rapids, Finkton, Kearney, Mancelona, Mitchell, Mount Bliss, Rockery, Snowflake, Spencer Creek, Stover, Torch Lake, and Wetzel. There was no mention of the little Indian village of Kewadin.

The village, located on the north end of Elk Lake, was originally known as the We-qua-ge-mog. Head of the Indian population was a chieftain named Ke-way-din, which, translated into the Chippewa language, meant "northwest wind." It was for him the village was named.

Ke-way-din was one of the last of the pure-blooded Chippewa Indian chieftains. He died early in the winter of 1884 and was buried with all of the tribal pomp and ceremony possible in that day.

At the time of his death, Ke-way-din was believed to be far past a hundred years of age. He said he fought under the British flag in the last war, along with Aish-qua-guan-a-ba, one of the five chieftains over the Chippewa Indians in the Michigan-Wisconsin area.

On his death he was buried in the Indian cemetery (unmarked grave) at Kewadin, and with him was buried all of those things which denoted his rank and rule.

The deceased chief was dressed neatly for burial and, with him in his coffin was placed, in addition to a large amount of artificial flowers, his hunting knife, corn for planting in the spirit world, cloth for a tent, and extra collars in case those he wore should become soiled during the long journey. Another item was a long strap with a hook on the end. This was for his use should he come close to the walls of the Happy Hunting Ground and be unable to scale them.

Kewadin is no longer an Indian settlement, although a portion of the residents is of aboriginal American blood. Recent years have brought about an upsurge of interest among the Indians in the presentation of their nature art and culture. Those remaining in the little community work diligently to revive and preserve a lost way of life.

KINGSLEY
WAS BORN OF THE RAILS

The village of Kingsley came into being with the arrival of the rails, and was named for one of the earliest settlers, Judson W. Kingsley.

In fact, Kingsley was created by the efforts of one man who saw a future in the rich land of the area and in the heavy stands of hardwood.

Dr. Myron S. Brownson opened an office in the village in 1874, after serving with the 188th New York Volunteer Regiment in the Civil War. He came to the area from Dansville, New York, where he had been practicing medicine.

The magnitude of the work done by Dr. Brownson in creating a village is almost beyond description.

After locating and establishing a successful practice, he purchased 1,000 acres of wooded property where the village now stands, and erected the first mill. He operated his own gristmill and built the first blacksmith

shop. The property he purchased was subsequently platted into the present village.

He erected two additional mills, and built 53 houses and business blocks in the village.

In 1900 he built a modern flour mill known as the "Toner Roller Mill" and was instrumental in the erection of the Methodist church. In addition to his contribution toward the construction of the Methodist church, Dr. Brownson also contributed toward the erection of churches of other denominations.

At the turn of the century, Dr. Brownson, in addition to owning about 1,000 acres of land, had 400 acres under cultivation.

Although Kingsley was a "one man town" in its beginnings, it is now a model rural village. The ground work laid by kindly Dr. Brownson has continued to weather the years. In recent times there has been indication that Kingsley will continue to grow and prosper. It is a typical rural village, friendly and expansive; always extending a hand of friendship to guests or travelers.

LAKE ANN
REFUSED TO DIE

Lake Ann, smallest incorporated village in the state of Michigan, refused to quit.

The loss of the lumber industry failed to halt its progress. In spite of the depletion of the rolling acres of timber and a disasterous fire, the village seemed to prosper.

There was a possibility, at one time, early in the 1890's, that Lake Ann would out distance Traverse City in its bid as the capital city in the Grand Traverse Region.

Dreams were shattered, however, in 1897 when a roaring fire destroyed the entire village. The flames, starting in the William Habbler mill on the shore of Lake Ann, swept through the dry flame business buildings like a whirlwind. Firemen from Traverse City and from other areas rushed to the aid of the village, but it was in vain.

But Lake Ann rebuilt. Despite the fact that there was only an approximate $10,000.00 insurance policy on the entire business and residential district, the property owners were a determined lot.

But it was not in the overall plan that Lake Ann should resume its place in the growing number of prosperous villages in the region.

In 1914, another disasterous fire destroyed most of the business section. The houses and business structures were not so well built as before and there was a considerable accumulation of slabwood and other material which added to the flames. The fact that the village buildings were more scattered saved a portion.

Following the 1914 fire, there was only a small amount of rebuilding. The village had lost its bid for a place in the industrial or business horizon.

In 1918, fire once more took a toll and the people of Lake Ann lost determination. The residents ceased to dream of a teeming city and settled down to enjoy the fact that their village had a future as a resort community.

Today it is just that . . . a charming village on the shores of a beautiful lake . . . with no dream of competing for industry or highrise apartments.

LAKE LEELANAU
HAD AN EARLY OIL BOOM

One of the earliest settlers in the area now embracing the village of Lake Leelanau, a village in Leelanau county, was A. De Belloy.

While not the first settler in the village, De Belloy gave the community the widest possible publicity when he organized the Grand Traverse Bay Mineral Land Association in 1867 and drilled a well in search of oil.

The exploration failed to find oil, but, at a depth of 700 feet, a splendid flow of mineral water was tapped. The well was publicized as having medicinal qualities and people came from far and wide to haul away jugs, decanters, and kegs of it.

First called the "Narrows" because of its location on the bottleneck of Lake Leelanau, the village, as it grew, was called Provemont. Later, to associate the village with the lake on which it was located, the name was changed to Lake Leelanau.

For many years Provemont, and later Lake Leelanau, was the banking center of the county. There was a grist mill, saw mill, several stores, and the village was a shopping center for a large portion of the county.

Located on the Manistee and Northeastern Railroad, the village had a vast potential. For a time there was a hustle that was indicative of a great future, but, with the closing of the timber industries and the coming of the automobile, Lake Leelanau became another country village.

Yet, industrious people, good business planning, and an influx of summer people gave the village a new lease on life.

One of the vitalizing developments in the community was the establishment of a convent and school by the Sisters of St. Dominic, later and presently, Dominican Sister.

Provemont was primarily a settlement of French pioneers with a scattering of Bohemian and Polish. An area of agricultural land just south of the village was known, for many years, as "Polackville," "Polltown," and by other and similar names because of a concentration of Polish settlers.

Today Lake Leelanau is as pretty a village as can be found in the region. It has grown from a sprawling lumbering town to a modern, 20th century village. Modern buildings and progressive people have given life to what might well have been a ghost town.

LELAND
"FISH TOWN" TO MOST OF US

In 1848, two easterners, Antoine Manseau and John I. Miller, explored northern Michigan for a practical site for a mill. They located a spot at the mouth of the Carp river (Leland river), but made no improvements until 1853 when Manseau and his son, Antoine, built a mill on the river.

In September of 1853, Miller returned and settled on his holdings, located a short distance north of the river. He erected a store and was appointed first postmaster of the village. In 1859, Miller sold to Cordes and Thies who erected a saw mill and grist mill and constructed a dock.

Rev. Fr. Mrack, Catholic missionary to the Indians, held first religious services in the village and, in 1870, the Holy Trinity church was erected.

In 1869, a group of Detroit business men decided Leland was an excellent place for operation of an iron furnace. The buildings and kilns were erected and

operation started the following year. The firm was known as The Leland Lake Superior Iron Company and employed a large force of men.

The production of iron, however, was never profitable and the firm spent its capital of $150,000.00 within a two year period. In 1872 the plant was sold to Captain E. B. Ward and Company. Assuming an indebtedness of $100,000.00, however, was too much. Two disasterous fires contributed to the closing of the milll.

The heavy blow dealt by failure of the iron smelter did not erase Leland from the map.

In 1881, the county seat of Leelanau county was removed from Northport to Leland. The *Enterprise,* oldest paper in Leelanau county, also moved from Northport in 1883 and has since remained at Leland.

A fishing harbor (Fish Town) and modern harbor of refuge has contributed much to the industrial revenue at Leland and has continued to add materially to its importance as a Mecca for tourists.

MANCELONA
IT HAS A GIRL'S NAME

Land was selling at from $7.00 to $10.00 an acre when Perry Andress arrived, with his family, in 1869. His choice of location was in Antrim county where a level plateau gave promise of good farming land. He erected a hotel on his land and the village, thus born, was named after his daughter Mancelona Andress.

Mancelona was given its next commercial building in 1872 when L.C. Handy and A.D. Carpenter arrived to the site of Mancelona and erected a general store, establishing the nucleus of a business district.

Handy was an aggressive leader in the young village and set about securing industry. It was his efforts which caused to be established a "butter dish factory," later to become the giant Oval Wood Dish Company of Traverse City, still operating at Tupper Lake, New York.

A.D. Carpenter, who arrived with Handy, operated a store in Boyne City for some time and later returned

to Mancelona to enter a partnership with Handy in his store.

A second store was built shortly after the Handy enterprise came into being. Marshall Emery arrived about 1874 and opened a general store which, with the Handy business, constituted the only mercantile operations in the village for many years.

Soon after the arrival of Handy and Carpenter, the village was designated a post office and Perry Andrus was named to the position of postmaster. He held the assignment for about a year and was followed by L.C. Handy.

Centrally located in Antrim county, Mancelona, since the pioneer days, has been the business center of the area. Its shopping center has maintained a steady growth and its people have been progressive.

Farming, while a considerable item in the Mancelona economy, is not the only source of income. Located in close proximity to many lakes and streams, although not directly on any body of water, it has become a focal point for thousands of vacation-minded people.

MAPLE CITY
THEY CALLED IT "PEGTOWN"

Centrally located in Leelanau County, Maple City owes its birth and existence to the heavy stands of hardwood timber which once covered the land.

Kasson township, in which the little village is located, was named for Kasson Freeman, government surveyor. The only major industry, the manufacturing of wooden pegs for shoes, was first established by William H. Crowell.

Because of this thriving industry, the village was known for many years as "Pegtown." The tiny hardwood pegs were used by shoemakers and shipped across the nation. The coming of metal nails, however, brought an end to the industry.

Replacing the peg factory was a new partnership when Crowell went into the sawmill business with Adam Bellinger and the mill was known as the Crowell and Bellinger mill.

With the coming of a postoffice to the village, it was

necessary to decide on a more fitting name. First it was called Maple and, subsequently, as today, called Maple City.

Crowell and Bellinger mill continued to operate long after many of the other mills had closed. They installed machinery for the manufacture of flooring and entered a new field in the production of wooden dishes such as butterbowls. These dishes were manufactured in several sizes and were shipped all over the middle west.

The peg factory closed down in 1876 when a final shipment of wooden pegs remained unsold at a metropolitan market. It was about this time that the village of Maple City could well have disappeared from the map.

As the forest retreated under the woodman's axe and saw, the area around Maple City became agricultural. Homesteaders, those who were able to weather the rigors of pioneering deprivation, began to prosper. The beautiful lakes of the area attracted summer guests and vacation minded people from metropolitan centers.

In this community, as well as several others in the Grand Traverse region, there were fine stands of cedar which remained after the hardwood was gone. Cedar shingles and posts from this timber was a boon to the struggling village.

MAYFIELD ADVERTISING PAID OFF

Circulars and advertisements in the papers in the middle east can be credited with the settlement of the village of Mayfield, located in a pretty valley between Traverse City and Kingsley.

During the days following the Civil War, there was need for "land seekers" and settlers in order to keep the passenger traffic booming on the Great Lakes. The Grand Traverse Region was one of the places extolled.

First settlers in Mayfield were the families of Albert Barnum, a cousin of the famous P.T. Barnum, and William Denniston.

Barnum homesteaded land on a hill overlooking the present village. Denniston chose land a bit farther to the south. The settlement of these families, however, did not actually begin the village. It was the construction of a mill on the little creek which cuts through the valley.

In 1868, Messrs. Gibbs, Knight, and Neal built a sawmill and Denniston erected a general store which housed the postoffice. The village was called Beulah. The name of the postoffice was, however, Mayfield ... and Mayfield it remained. Below the sawmill, Neal, Gibbs, and Company built a grist mill and, in 1872, the rails connected the village with Traverse City.

About 1872 (date uncertain), Israel Dawdy built a hotel which was known as the Dawdy House.

The hill to the west of the present village provided an ideal rollway area for logs and the mill did an excellent business. The first cut was with an old style muley saw: vertical gangs working like bucksaws. Later, when circular saws were installed, the village prospered. A shingle mill was erected and the future looked bright for Mayfield.

The lumbering industry suddenly died and the major industry found little raw material with which to work. Fire destroyed the mill and it was rebuilt, only to be destroyed again.

Mayfield is a pretty little village with a quiet, rural atmosphere. Hidden among the wooded hills, it is a pleasant retreat from the hustle of modern living.

MESICK
A YOUNG VILLAGE

Old records make no mention of the village of Mesick. Not even Page's book, *The Traverse Region*, published in 1884, makes mention of the town.

The reason is simple: Mesick is a young town, as ages of communities are figured. It was platted in 1890 and incorporated in 1902.

The village of Mesick was never entirely dependent on the lumbering industry for holding its own in a struggle for existence. Built, as it was, on the route of the Ann Arbor railroad, it grew rapidly and was a banking center for the community as well as an important shopping center.

The village was named for the Howard Mesick family, pioneers. Mesick, a native of New York, came west to try his hand at making a fortune. He was a farmer, sailed the lakes, worked in the timber, and, with the help of one man, cut 36 miles of roadway through the wildrness from Traverse City to Otsego Lake.

He finally settled in the Mesick community where he owned 160 acres of land.

Following the incorporation of the village in 1902, an election of town officers was held. R.M.Harry was elected president; and F.E. Rice was named village clerk. W.W. Galloway was voted into the office of treasurer, and B.C. Halstead was elected assessor.

Sherman, near by, long a thriving village, showed indications that it would absorb the Mesick business as well as that in the village of Wexford. Wexford fell victim to the situation, but Mesick continued to prosper.

Despite the fact that it was located off the direct route from Traverse City to Cadillac, it managed to survive the lumber slump.

Today the village has an enviable position in the Grand Traverse Bay Region picture. Its location on the Manistee river and the giant backwater of the Hodenpyle dam offers attractive vacation sites.

Mesick village officials have been progressive. The town supports a very active Chamber of Commerce and joins in all promotions which are beneficial to the region.

NORTHPORT
BECAUSE OF REV. SMITH

The village of Northport had its beginning, as did so many pioneer villages, in the conviction of an individual to do missionary work among the Indians. Rev. George Nelson Smith arrived at what is now the site of the village of Northport on June 11, 1849. Rev. Smith had booked passage aboard the schooner *H. Merrill* which was owned by James McLaughlin.

McLaughlin had been ordered to work with the Indians in the Grand Traverse Region. In booking passage on the *H. Merrill*, Rev. Smith brought with him his wife, Arvilla, and four children. The total pioneer party consisted of 15 men, women and children.

The first house in the village was located on the bank of the tiny creek which runs through the village, and the house was later used, for many years, as a general store.

The Waukazoo band of Indians, consisting of between 40 to 50 families, received their name from a

leader, Chief Waukazoo, and the present village of Northport was first called Waukazooville. It was later changed to Northport. Even today one of the main streets of the village is named Waukazoo.

Rev. Smith passed away on April 5, 1881, and was buried near his home on the bank of the creek and in the soil he had loved so dearly. For a while the village of Waukazooville (Northport) was restricted in growth by the creation of the Indian reservation to the south. Only a small point of land to the north was available for exploitation. The term of the reservation expired in 1886 and Northport grew.

Northport was organized into a school district in 1855, the first in what is now Leelanau county. A postoffice was established in 1855 and the village was incorporated in 1903 with Wilber E. Campbell as first president.

OMENA
NEW MISSION

Nearly hidden in a cluster of trees, serene on a gentle hill, is a tiny church in the village of Omena. It is around this little Presbyterian house of worship that more than a century of history is written.

In the cemetery adjacent to the church lie the bodies of pioneers and Indians who helped bring the quiet village into being. There is buried the body of Chief Ahgosa.

The village had its beginning in 1852 when Reverend Peter Dougherty decided to remove his mission church from the tip of the Old Mission peninsula in Grand Traverse Bay and relocate it at the present site of Omena. For some time the location was called New Mission.

At the time of the removal to New Mission, the point was occupied by a small group of Indians of Shawb-wah-sun's band. These early native people remained as a part of the new church development.

The New Mission church bell is of great interest to visitors in the community. It is made from copper alloy, using large British pennies which the natives collected and contributed.

The Reverend Dougherty built a school at New Mission, teaching both trade and general courses. Many of the Chippewa Indians, who came across from Old Mission, were located near the Indian mission at Peshabestown, a Catholic mission for Ottowa Indians. There was a gradual intermingling of the tribes until, today, there are very few Indians of pure blood remaining.

New Mission never was a bustling community insofar as commerce or industry are concerned. From the very beginning it was a Christian mission and a vacation area.

Today it is a pleasant rural village and a haven for summer guests. There is a postoffice, small business section, and a beautiful beach on Omena bay.

RAPID CITY
CHANGED FROM "VAN BUREN"

In the south quarter of section nine, town 28 north, range eight, west, Kalkaska county, lies the quiet village of Rapid City.

The village was first platted about 1890 and subsequently added to when Charles E. VanBuren moved his store from Clement's Corners (two miles east) to the present site of the village.

After the arrival of VanBuren, the village was given a postoffice and service was started on November 22, 1892, with Charles VanBuren as the first postmaster. He was postmaster until July 11, 1893 when Daniel McAlpine was appointed.

The name of the village was officially listed as VanBuren on January 18, 1895 and Andrew Anderson was named postmaster.

Again the name was changed on April 30, 1898 when it was decided to call it Rapid City, after the swift

little river which flows nearby. The first postmaster after this change was Thomas G. Anderson.

During those years, there was intensive lumbering inustry all around the village site. The Chicago and Northwestern railroad came through the area and two spurs served the Rapid City community. A cooperate mill turned out hoops and staves, there was one large mill and several smaller ones operating near the village.

The platting of the village shows several street names which even the residents of the community may have forgotten. The names of the old streets are Van-Buren, Water, River, Stall, Main, Church, Elm, and South.

The newspapers flourished in the village at one period in its history. One, The *Rapid River Rustler,* was published by R. J. Ribblett (Old Rib) and the other, The *Rapid City News,* much smaller, lived briefly at a later date.

The oldest active business in the village was the Mirage general store, built in 1896, more recently destroyed by fire. The old rail spurs are gone and the trees are second and third growth. Rapid City, however, is the focal point for fishermen and hunters. Too, it entertains an excellent summer resort business.

SOUTH BOARDMAN
FIRE STOPPED THIS CITY

The little village of South Boardman, located just off highway 131 in Kalkaska county, was once a bustling community of over 1,500 people. It was a busy place when lumber was the major commodity in so many northern towns.

A series of fires at the turn of the century and then, in 1921, the big one, all but removed the little town from the map. The big Anderson mill, the hotel, post office, restuarant, three stores, and several other structures were destroyed.

The fire which destroyed the town was caused by a cigarette which was tossed from a window of the village poolhall.

The late Alvin Ellis recalled that, when he came to South Boardman in 1902, there were four churches and five saloons active. At that time the mill was cutting from 90,000 to 120,000 feet of lumber a day and no

one had given a thought to the supply ever being exhausted.

Main street in South Boardman, which runs north and south, and Traverse street, which runs east and west, were lined with shops and stores and the hotel did a bustling business both from traveling men and from the lumbermen on a quite occasional spree.

The town never really recovered from its destruction. The postoffice remained for several years and a scattering of small businesses readjusted to the destruction. However, the lumber business waned and the big mill was never rebuilt.

A small stream, the south branch of the Boardman river from which the town received its name, supplied sufficient waterhead to run a small turbine mill and this remained operative until recent years.

U.S. 131, which skirts the village on the west, has provided an incentive for a scattering of new business ventures. However, there are few who believe South Boardman will ever see a rebirth of its early glory.

Yet, while traffic scoots by on the modern highway, there seems to be serenity about the place that invites a passerby to spend a few minutes ... or days ... enjoying the quiet and restful atmosphere.

SUMMIT CITY
DIED WITH THE TIMBER

"Summit City never had a chance," said an oldtimer in talking about the pioneer settlement. "There was only the lumbering and related industry to keep it alive and when that was gone, so was Summit City."

How the village got its name is not a matter of record. It was platted in the northwest quarter of the northwest quarter of section 22, Paradise township.

The Traverse City branch of the Grand Rapids and Indiana railroad was incentive for the establishment of the Michigan Flooring and Handle Manufacturing Company.

The timber caused the opening of a store and hardware business, establishment of a church, and the organization of social groups in the village.

It was June 23, 1874, that a postoffice was opened at Summit City. Joseph A. Swainston was named first postmaster and held the post for only a little over a

month. A. J. Albright was named to succeed Swainston and he was in office for three years.

There was a succession of eight postmasters until May 14, 1955 when the office was discontinued with all mail being distributed from the Kingsley office. Ruth Kyselka was the last to hold the office in the Summit City postoffice.

While the big flooring and handle plant in the village was a business incentive, employing about 30 persons, there was plenty of timber activity before that. Mills in the surrounding area brought boarding houses into being and gave business to the stores. Actually, the Michigan Flooring and Handle Manufacturing Company did not operate until February, 1884, 10 years after the postoffice had been opened.

Located as the village was, in the heart of a level farming area, the agricultural development gave promise of a fair future for the settlement. This was shortlived, however, because of the nature of the soil, light and unfertile, failed to support intensive production.

Today there is but a small concentration of homes where Summit City was once located.

Considerable stands of hard maple provide a minor industry in the community in the production of maple syrup and hundreds of acres have been reforested and set to evergreen trees for Christmas harvest.

SUTTONS BAY
THREE NAME CHANGES

The village of Suttons Bay has gone through three changes of name, but never has there been a change in its friendly people or in its beautiful location. The village was first laid out by Fr. A. Herbstrit, a missionary priest, in 1871. His hope was to build a Catholic church, school, college, and found a Catholic settlement. He failed in all but the church and school. He named his fledgling village Pleasantville City.

Actually, the town was to have been named in honor of H.C. Sutton, first owner of the land on which it is located. In 1865, the location was known as Suttonsburg and the development of Pleasantville City, almost within its limits, was doomed to failure because of the expansion of Suttonsburg.

At the end of 1879, the settlement, by that time known as Suttons Bay, boasted more than 250 residents. It had four general stores, two hotels, a sawmill, and half a dozen smaller businesses.

123

One of the colorful eras in the history of Suttons Bay was the publication of the *Suttons Bay Bazoo*, a paper which made its appearance occasionally under the guiding but not too tactful hand of Sam Cooley. The *Suttons Bay Tribune* kept the world informed of the early activities in the village, and during the 1880's, was succeeded by the *Sentinel*. Later the *Courier* continued the tradition of local and regional news.

Suttons Bay is, like so many villages in the Grand Traverse region, a vacation spot. The waters of the bay, which opens into Lake Michigan, offer much to boating enthusiasts. Fishing, both winter and summer, offers another major attraction.

Because of its location between a ridge of glacial hills and the bay, Suttons Bay has come to be known as the Alpine Village of the Grand Traverse region. It is known across the middlewest as a restful community, with a dignity born of the pioneers.

THOMPSONVILLE
HENRY WARD BEECHER HELPED

There is no village in the north which so thoroughly owes its beginning to the lumber industry as does Thompsonville.

There was the Thompson Lumber Company, Sands Lumber Company, Judson Lumber Company, Buckley and Douglas, and several others of lesser magnitude, all operating in that area of Benzie county.

The village is located in two townships, Colfax and Weldon. The east side of the village, in Colfax township, was swampy and most of the early business places moved to the Weldon (west) side of the road.

The first settlers arrived in 1880, and the first real lumbering activity was started by the family of the famous revivalist, Henry Ward Beecher. In fact, the east part of the village was known as "Beecher's Side" for years.

The village grew rapidly and was incorporated late

in the year of 1891. The first village election was held on January 11, 1892.

In 1898 the village was far from a dry town. There were 13 saloons operating full blast.

The railroad brought the first easy public access to the community. First there were the rails of the Chicago and West Michigan, later purchased by Pere Marquette, and later by the Chesapeake and Ohio. The second railroad to enter the village was the Frankfort and Southeastern, which only went as far south as Copemish and connected with the Manistee and Northeastern. Later (about 1895) the Ann Arbor took over.

With the rails in town, they needed a name for the depot. Residents were toying with the name Nuack until, one night, someone put up a sign "Thompsonville." No one thought to credit the prank to a member of the Thompson family who owned the big Thompson Lumber Company.

Thompsonville isn't growing rapidly. The residents are happy in the quiet and friendly surroundings of an agricultural and winter sports community.

TORCH RIVER
IT WAS FIRST "PERSONS HARBOR"

One of the newer villages in the Grand Traverse region is the pleasant community of Torch River. Located on the river of the same name, half in the county of Kalkaska and half in Antrim, it enjoys a bustling summer business.

The first plat was surveyed in 1903 when George W. Persons purchased 40 acres of land and laid out what he hoped would be a town of some importance.

Because, of his name, and the location of the village on the shores of Torch Lake, the name Persons Harbor was the first designation.

The same year another plat was surveyed when Otto Ameisegger broke another 40 acres into village lots. The Persons plat was on the Antrim county side of the river and the Ameisegger plat was in Kalkaska.

For some years the village remained undeveloped and thinly populated. There was a shambles of a bridge

across the river to the west of the village, later replaced by a barge ferry, operated jointly by the two counties.

In 1929, Walter Watson and Frank Riggs purchased 80 acres of land from the Dexter and Noble empire in Elk Rapids and another village plat was laid out.

The community, however, never reached village stature. There was never a postoffice and no officers were ever elected.

Yet, there was progressive business. Henry H. Rice, one of the pioneers of the area, built a general store in 1909 and operated it for 36 years. The river has always sustained a great boating program and the attending boat business.

The first house in the community was a small (16 x 20), shed-roof structure which H.J. Bingham moved in from Kalkaska. It took two days and the crew was forced to remove stumps along the way to allow passage of the building. Bingham later erected and operated the Bingham hotel which was razed in 1960.

TRAVERSE CITY
CAPITAL OF THE NORTH

Traverse City, capital of the north, had its beginnings in 1847 when a doughty old farmer in Napierville, Illinois, Captain Boardman, purchased a small tract of land at the mouth of the Boardman River.

More than a century has passed and Traverse City has never hesitated in its stride forward. From the first tiny, hewn-log house at the corners of Boardman avenue and East Eighth street to the modern and beautiful city, has been reflected progress. Exact location of the first house was in the right-hand, right-of-way, looking east on Eighth street, just east of the traffic control light.

From this pioneer beginning has grown a fine city.

Where the present courthouse now stands, was an ancient burial ground, and just to the south of that was once a more modern burial plot. When Captain Boardman arrived in the region, there were a number of graves on the bank of the river just west of Boardman

school and there was a small Indian village just south of that.

Like the hub of a wheel, Traverse City has become the center of trade for the Greater Grand Traverse Region.

The city is blessed with one of the most modern medical centers in the middle west. Its merchants are as progressive as can be found.

The climate of the area is moderate, favored by the warming waters of Grand Traverse Bay . . . cool breezes in summer and mild winter climate.

In Traverse City are friendly people who have made industry of the summer vacation trade. They have found a way of welcome that has become known across the nation.

WILLIAMSBURG
MOVED ... AND LIVED

The old flouring mill still stands and the ancient dam still holds a head of water. But no flour is produced and the stones have long since been idle. The property, scenic and memory filled, is privately owned and well maintained.

Williamsburg, located just off M-72 and east of the village of Acme, was first given breath in 1856 when three families settled on tiny Mill creek. In rapid succession, other families settled in the area and a mill was erected by Kossuth Stites and A. W. Eaton.

To the older residents of the village, there could never be a permanent town. They were more certain when the highway was changed and the "oldtown" was abandoned.

But the business interests moved with the highway and the village still lived and prospered. In later years the road was again re-routed and the town left isolated.

But it has made little difference. There is still a post-office and general stores. There is no indication that Williamsburg will die.

There is a nostalgic reason for a drive here and there through the village. Ask an oldtimer about "Buttermilk Corners" and he will tell you about the creamery at the intersection of the village road and M-72. Look at the still remaining footings of the business block buildings.

The church in the old village is still a place of worship and reflects the hardiness of the people who founded Williamsburg. It was built with volunteer labor and from contributed materials.

When the rails first arrived in Williamsburg, there was an overpass trestle. With the construction of the sawmill by Stites and Eaton, the trestle was moved and a grade crossing was constructed.

A walk through the old cemetery, located in the heart of the village, is like skipping through pages of a colorful hstory book. There lie the wonderful folks who first opened the wilderness farm community.

Of recent times, a new and different pioneer has invaded the quiet community. The search for oil far beneath the wooded acres and the adjacent farm land has been a disruption unwelcome to many. Yet, it is a part of progress and has, in no manner, spoiled the natural beauty of the Williamsburg community.

Many members of the Williams family, for whom the community was named, still live in the Grand Traverse region.

So, as you wander about the bay area, take time to leave the beaten path. Take the short drive on "old 72" and see for yourself what it is like to visit a still peaceful and quiet town, reminiscent of a century ago.

BARNESTORMING THE GRAND TRAVERSE BAY REGION

Pine forest stretched for miles on end, and the rolling beauty of the Grand Traverse Bay region could not be seen for the beauty of the forest. There was hardwood: gigantic maple, beech, birch, black cherry and seemingly endless miles of pine. Only here and there was there open space where wild daisies and wild blackberries and raspberries grew in abundance. Over most of the forest-covered hills there was the ever bountiful blueberry.

Through all of the glorious outdoors there was seldom a voice other than those of the loon or the elk or the dawnsong of the wildbird or the nightcall of the owl.

Paths frequently criss-crossed the Grand Traverse Bay region: footpaths to enable the native people, the Ottawas and Chippewas, to move on their frequent migrations.

It will probably never be known for sure who were the first white men to walk in the Grand Traverse region. There is speculation, books have been written. We know that Father Marquette crossed the mouth of the Grand Traverse

Bay, and we know that the British and French adventurers approached from the north.

Who was the first we can only speculate. We are positive, of course, that Bishop Barraga was an early visitor and that Father Mrack spent some time in the region on business of his church.

Too, we are reasonably sure that unidentified fur traders ventured both north and south, for this was the land of the otter, the beaver, the mink, and the muskrat.

Of course, in those early days of the Grand Traverse region, there were no roads. Only footpaths connected the far reaches of the communities; paths marked, not by blazing a tree, but by bending hardwood saplings in the direction of the pathway.

The saplings were weighted down by rocks or fallen logs and grew in a short but lazy sort of "N" shape. Only one good specimen of a trail-marker tree still lives in the area around Traverse City. It is located in what was formerly the Grand Traverse county fairgrounds.

Major trails in the region led from Cross Village, near Petoskey, from the Leelanau Peninsula, and from Old Mission Point. They converged on Traverse City and the trails then led to different locations: Manistee, Grand Rapids, Detroit and other important settlements.

That there were people in the Grand Traverse Bay region long before history was recorded, there is little doubt. Where the Grand Traverse county courthouse was built workmen unearthed an ancient mound. There is little reason to doubt that the mound was Hopewellian in its origin, and that the builders were related in some manner to those who built the great mounds in Ohio.

Artifacts removed from the mound, commonly referred to as "Jail Hill," were not preserved. There is written record of the items and minor classifications was done, but no trace of them has been found since shortly after they were discovered.

Also, there are remains of arrow and spearhead manufactories in the area. These are found from Mackinaw City southward, including the Grand Traverse Region.

139

Indian warfare in the Grand Traverse region has always been a controversial subject among amateur as well as professional historians. The difficulty of separating fact from fiction leaves the "war" and the "no-war" forces widely separated.

Most historians, however, believe that there was never a serious conflict this side of Mackinaw City. There is a story of a battle of a small tribe of Musquetaw (spelling variable) Indians and a band of Ottawas. Connected with this legend is a story of buried gold of an uncertain amount. However, the true story will never be known.

In the overall picture, the Indians of the Grand Traverse region were a peaceful people, undoubtedly more so than the swarms of white folks who came in the 1800's, first in small groups, then in droves, to lay waste the virgin timber and pollute the land.

In the summer of 1839, Reverend Peter Dougherty, a graduate of Princeton Theological Seminary, visited what was later to be called the Old Mission in Peninsula township. A missionary, he planned to establish a school and church at the tip of the peninsula.

In May of the following year, he returned from his base at Mackinaw City and, with the aid of the Indians, constructed a bark shack, the first step in the establishment of a church and a school. The original Dougherty home, built to replace the bark structure, still stands at Old Mission, and is appropriately marked with a bronze plaque.

The old church building, too, has been rebuilt and remains as a monument to the first white settler in the entire Grand Traverse Bay region.

And the years passed. Much important history was lost because it was never recorded. Old diaries and ledgers have helped in the preservation of the history and historical points of the region.

It is the purpose of this work to show you some of the almost forgotten monuments to those who believed in the land, in their own ability, and in the future of this wonderful country.

The tours presented in the following pages are as nearly accurate as research can make them. Most of the sites are near highways while others may be a little distance one way or another. Not much, mind you, but please remember that the people who created these points of interest were not planning tours or expecting sightseers.

TOUR NUMBER ONE

This little drive will take you through the beginnings of Traverse City. Remember that Perry Hannah, A. Tracy Lay, Mike Oberlin, Thomas "Titmouse" Bates, and scores of other pioneers walked the ground over which we will drive. Enjoy our directions as we "Barnestorm" through the Grand Traverse Region.

At the Chamber of Commerce building, 202 Grandview Parkway, we head north and turn right on the parkway. Here we start a drive over what was once "Squaw Point," a narrow point of land extending between Boardman river and the west arm of Grand Traverse Bay. It was here that the Indians came to camp, came in their dugout canoes and hunted while the squaws picked huckleberries or whatever they could forage for their tables. Here too was the railroad yards. The tracks came in back of what is now Murray's Boat Shop. This area was, at one time, solid railroad tracks.

Now we approach Bob Murchie Bridge, named for Robert Murchie, local attorney, who worked diligently for years to have the Grandview Parkway constructed. And ahead on your left was located the Wequetongsing Yacht

Club. The river mouth entered near where the Holiday Inn is now located, and the river was crossed to the club on a board footpath suspended barely above the water.

At the traffic light just over the bridge we turn back directly west on East Front street. Remember that in the days of the pioneers, when Perry Hannah, A. Tracy Lay, and Captain Boardman first came here, the original buildings, the business block, was built on this street and all of the buildings faced the water. There were no buildings on the south side of the street.

As we pass Wellington street, the first schoolhouse was constructed where you see a little sewing shop, The Bobbin Shop (1975). That is one of the Hannah-Lay additions to the village of Traverse City. The first schoolhouse was an abandoned log stable which was used for several years with one schoolteacher, Helen Goodale, who walked from the Hannah and Lay boarding house on the other side of the river to teach school. Sometimes she skipped across the river on logs.

We are now approaching the business section proper, and it was along this street, on the left hand side, that the original boarding houses were erected. Several of them were built, and then as property became more difficult to find for ideal building sites, the right hand side, or the north side of the street was commercialized.

We are now approaching what was originally the site of an early boarding house on the left. A gigantic masonry bank building, National Bank and Trust, has been erected on its site.

Note the State Theater (233 E. Front). It was here that the Steinberg Opera House was constructed in 1896 and became a social focal point of the community. It later burned and some of the seats were removed and placed in theaters. It was here that the repertoire companies assembled and offered the finest talent of the era.

Now, on the left, we see the Hamilton Clothing Company, a century old. Mr. Hamilton worked for Mr. Perry Hannah in the mercantile business and, one day, Hannah asked him if he didn't think he was smart enough to start his own business. He thought competition was good, and would furnish financial help for Hamilton. Next to Hamilton's is the Milliken's Store (204 E. Front). That too is a century old.

Across the street on the right you see a masonry building called the Beadle Building. Mr. Beadle directed this building, installed his harness shop here and made harnesses. He also sold carriage supplies. This was after the turn of the century, and after that, business began scattering along Front street on both sides.

On the left you now see a little yellow building with the word "Sleder" up at the top. Here was the Sleder Meat Market and for many, many years a family tradition— Sleder's Meats. Nobody, nobody, could produce and sell the meats of the quality of Sleder's.

Next to Sleder's was the old A & P store, now an arcade (140 E. Front). It was during depression days that Eddie Hallberg operated the store.

On the left, ahead of us, we see Petertyl's Drug Store and adjacent to it, the old Anderson Building (116 E. Front). It was in the basement of the Anderson Building that they had "Hans Hurry Back," a saloon. Here was a gathering place for what was referred to sometimes as the "toughs" of the community and many a fight, it if were a matter of record, could be recounted in this area.

On the right was the old Hannah and Lay Mercantile, constructed with the exception of the front fascade, from bricks manufactured in the Grand Traverse region. The bricks were taken from Markham's Brickyard in Leelanau county.

On the left is the Masonic building; that too was constructed from bricks taken from the Markham's Brickyard on the banks of Cedar Lake.

Now we are going into a block which was not developed until later. Sawdust from the "Big Mill," which we will identify later as to location, was piped across here and today, when construction takes place, the excavation brings up piles of half-rotted sawdust, dormant here for a century.

As we cross the Boardman river once again, we notice Fochtman Motor Company on the right. It was directly across from this building that the first mill was constructed, when Captain Horace Boardman and Michael Gay arrived in 1847. The mill was a "muley" with one saw and operated from a pit using a saw which operated on an eccentric . . . not the circular saw which was to come into use at a later date.

Later the mill moved a few hundred feet upstream, where a better head of water was available. The creek was, naturally, named Mill creek. Later it became known as Asylum creek and still later, was renamed Kids creek.

Ahead of us, at the traffic signal, is the main artery of traffic into Traverse City from the south, Division street. Across Division we continue to Elmwood avenue, where we turn right.

Elmwood avenue was the flight path of the passenger pigeons when they were so plentiful that they darkened the sky. It was presumed that the birds were following a pattern from their feeding grounds in Wisconsin to their nesting area in the "Elm Flats," which we will later visit.

Along Elmwood avenue, hunters would asssemble to shoot the birds for market, to club them, and to net them. Mark Craw, who was a boy at the time of the passenger pigeon flights, retold the story of how he used to carry ammunition from the Hannah, Lay and Company store when the hunters exhausted supplies. Nobody cared who shot which bird. They picked up the birds that fell, and there were enough for all.

This street (Elmwood) has, someplace along its route, a grave. Nobody knows who, nobody knows where, but in one of the front yards there lies the first white person to be buried, without service or ceremony, in the area. Stories have it that he was killed in a logging accident, and we're not exactly positive how accurate the information is.

We do know that this became one of the delightful residential areas . . . not an old one, but a middle class residential area which has been maintained and kept beautifully down through the years.

We are at the end of Elmwood and, directly across and to the right, on the bay, was one of the outstanding family business ventures and manufactories in the region. It was the Greilick Furniture Factory, located right on the water's edge. It was a steam operated mill. In later years it made furniture and still later, a modern line of children's furniture was manufactured before it was torn down.

We're now going down Bay Street, having turned right off Elmwood. This was the main artery along the bay prior to the creation of the boulevard. We're going to continue along Bay street across Division, and once again, we remind you that this is one of the main arteries into Traverse City from the south.

Directly across Division and on the right hand side, you'll see the Elks' lodge. This building was, at one time, the Osteopathic Hospital. When the hospital outgrew this building, it was sold to the Elks, a few conversions made inside, and now it is a very popular location.

Now we're coming into one of the early business sections of Traverse City. At the same time, we're entering what was known as "Slabtown." Here and back to the right, you'll notice several buildings that were originally stores. Some of the older ones have been torn down. That is Randolph street. Randolph street, while it still retains some of its businesses, has become a residential area to all intents and purposes.

We have turned left and we are back on Grandview Parkway, still going through what was once Slabtown. The little houses were built from slabs from the big mill. Slabtown started just a bit west of the railroad track crossing and went clear up to the mill. On our right we see the Rickerd Monument Works, which was the approximate location of Perry Hannah's first home in Traverse City. He lived in a tiny white house for many years before building his mansion on Sixth street.

On the left was the big mill, at the north end of Union street. After leaving the earlier location on Mill creek, they moved the mill to this spot and installed steam. Later the

Morgan Canning Company, one of the pioneers in processing of cherry products, built on a portion of the sight.

Across on the left, now, is Clinch Park Zoo, which was a city dump. The zoo was moved a number of years ago from a location directly across the parkway, now a great parking lot.

Now we're turning right on Cass Street (our point of beginning). Cross Front street. On the right again is the Beadle block and directly across is a vacant lot, which is a parking area for a medical clinic (116 Cass). Prokop Kyselka had his general store there, where he handled everything that was needed for the household, anything from crockery to lanterns to yardgoods.

The old firehouse on your right, a cream-colored brick building, was where the horse-drawn fire wagons were housed. Only recently (1975) was a new building constructed on West Front, to serve the downtown area with fire protection. Firemen for many years lived upstairs while the teams of horses were stabled on the first floor.

On the left was a business block, now Milliken's parking lot, and one of the first newspapers in the region was published almost exactly where the Milliken's sign is located in the parking lot.

We approach State street and across the street on the right-hand side is a red brick building which is now the city hall. It was once the postoffice. The postoffice was moved to a larger structure at State and Union streets. Adjacent and south is the police station. This was once the Ladies' Library building, one of the pioneer ladies organization in the region.

Now we cross the Boardman river again, and to the right of us we see a dam which was the site of Perry Hannah's grist mill. It operated for many years under the management of William Smith, and later burned to the ground. The dam has been maintained and is part of a park, which is a delightful place in which to spend an hour.

Now we turn right on Seventh street and we're going to go through an area in which the lumbermen built their beautiful homes at the turn of the century. They had the lumber; labor was an economy. No pains or money was spared in creating magnificent homes. We cross Union street and on your right you see a business area which was once a cemetery, the first cemetery in the Grand Traverse region. We will come back and take a closer look at this when we return on Sixth street.

We're now entering the area of lumberjack homes. On your left you'll see the old schoolhouse, which was once the high school for many years, more lately Central Elementary school.

Now observe the homes on the right. Many of them were built by lumbermen and businessmen. This was an isolated and quiet area at that time, you must remember.

We come to a stop street, which is Wadsworth, and we are now going down a lane of these beautiful homes. Turn right at Oak street and then right again at Sixth street.

Many of these homes had a third floor where they had a ballroom; we would call it a "rec" room today. In those days the ballroom was where the young people were taught social graces, and where the violin and concertina provided music.

You will please notice the porticos that stick out from some of the homes. It was here that the carriages stopped to pick up passengers. Then you will notice the pillars on many of the houses. Most of these pillars were hand made with elaborate gingerbread ornamenting the porches and entrances.

On the left, now, is the Carnegie Library, which was built at the turn of the century. The park on the left is named for Perry Hannah and was, at one time, an extremely beautiful area.

On the right is the beautiful Perry Hannah home (305 Sixth street). This home is built entirely of local materials, with the exception of one wood. The wiring is extremely inadequate in the house because the walls are anywhere from 18 inches thick and up, and of solid masonry. It is difficult, almost impossible, to rewire. The Hannah house is generally open to the public, as the present proprietor of the funeral home welcomes guests who wish to look at the magnificent workmanship in this old lumber baron home. Perry Hannah was known as the king of the "whitewater boys," and at an advanced age, he would go out on the river with the "river dogs" and ride the logs.

We are again nearing Union and will turn right. On your left is a part of the park that was once a burial ground for early settlers. When Hibbard's building (right) was first constructed many remains were unearthed. All were taken to Oakwood cemetery, where they were reinterred.

Now we're back on Union street, entering Oldtown. This was originally a sawdust street. Oldtown is, in many instances, just as it was 75 years ago.

On your right you see two buildings (402, 404 South Union) which formerly were cigar factories. The factories were called "buckeyes" because the owner would sit in the window and manufacture cigars; one eye on the cigar and one eye "out the window," as they would say, looking for a customer to whom they could sell cigars and maybe get permanent patrons.

You'll notice on both sides of the street the polyglot type of architecture. Most of it is as it was in "those days." Note the Wilhelm's store, which has been on the corner of Eighth and Union and in operation for almost a century, still maintaining the same business policies they had back in 1900.

Gas stations, however, have taken their toll of the old buildings. It is commonly called "progress."

We are passing Eighth street, and we're still on Union in Oldtown, moving past more business buildings. A few with new faces but, overall, still "as they were."

Cross Ninth street and you'll see on the left a pillared building (615 South Union), which was built by Herbert F. Boughey, a lumberman who, at one time, operated five mills in the Leelanau county. The entire building was built of local material and the third floor is trimmed entirely in birdseye maple.

We're turning left now on Tenth street and going by St. Francis Catholic church. Part of it has been rebuilt, especially the school, to accommodate the growth of the parish, but the old church at the corner of Cass and Tenth is still as it was 75 years ago. It was, at an earlier date, located across the street at 147 Tenth.

We're turning left on Cass street to head back to our point of beginning, and as we approach the next stoplight, you'll see a red masonry building which is the home of the Traverse City Civic Players. It was formerly the First Christian church.

On the left, ahead and through the light, you'll see a cream-colored building, the Traverse City Iron Works. It was also, at one time, the home of the R. G. Dunn cigar factory. It is amazing that the Traverse City Irons Works could remain through the century and offer no pollution to the beautiful Boardman river on the banks of which it is located. Nor is there any air pollution. The efficiency of the operation has contributed to its longevity.

We're on Cass and we're passing the Bo-Gi Club or youth center, formerly the old Grange Hall at the turn of the century. It was here farmers and their families talked out their problems and held social functions. Again we pass the city hall and the police department, back to our point of beginning at the Chamber of Commerce building.

We hope that you have enjoyed this tour, which has taken you through the early life-blood area of the city of Traverse City. Our next tour will take us to outlying areas within the city.

MILEAGE OF TOUR NUMBER ONE WAS APPROXIMATELY SEVEN MILES AND SHOULD TAKE ABOUT FORTY-FIVE MINUTES.

TOUR NUMBER TWO

Again we are at the Chamber of Commerce building. Incidentally, this building pays a dollar a year for what is called an "air and ground" lease from the city of Traverse City for permission to build the pedestal-type structure. The lease is negotiated every 30 years.

We turn left again on Grandview Parkway and pass the Clinch Park Zoo and recreational area with its beautiful beach and comprehensive museum. We pass the old Morgan cherry packing plant site, which is on the right at the end of Union street, indeed an historic spot.

Just beyond the former site of the Morgan plant, the large metal building you see is the city power plant, providing power to the municipality.

Once again we pass through the area that was known as Slabtown. It was here that Widder McGinnis was snowed in for one entire Christmas and missed her holiday because the snow had drifted over her house situated near the Rickerd Monument office and right next to the original Perry Hannah home.

Now we are passing the intersection of Division street and U.S. 31 and proceeding on to the junction of Bay street and Grandview Parkway. We point out that on the right was the old Greilick mill, first a sawmill and then a furniture factory.

Just beyond it you'll see some piling jutting out of the water, barely showing in some places. That was the location of the Darrow marina during World War II. The marina was later moved to the north edge of Greilickville. Now we approach the Westbay Shopping Center.

It was just in back of this section of business sites that the first hospital in the Grand Traverse region was established. It later burned to the ground. It was on the edge of the hill just behind the shopping center and was an institution with one nurse and one doctor. However, it contributed a great deal to the needs of the community.

We now leave the Grandview Parkway and turn sharp left and back onto Bay street. Again, we mention, this was the original and only access into Leelanau county and was once a dirt and sawdust trail.

We are approaching Elmwood avenue, where we will turn right. You will recall that in Tour One we pointed out that in the early part of the century the passenger pigeons used this for a "flyway," heading for the Elm Flats, where they roosted and nested by the hundreds and thousands. And, it was on this street where the unmarked grave of the first settler to die in Traverse City is located.

We follow Elmwood avenue and drive toward the State Hospital. Drive slowly and observe this beautiful middle class neighborhood. On the left you see a brick building boarded up on one end. That was the site of the old Elmwood school, razed when a new school was constructed.

We come to a stop street, which is West Front. Still on Elmwood, proceeding south and coming to Sixth street, cross Sixth and on your right you will see the Munson Medical Center. This is the medical capital of northern Michgan today. The road on which we're driving was the approximate site of the narrow-gauge railroad which came from the Markham Brickyard and brought the material from which the State Hospital buildings were constructed.

The State Hospital had, at one time, one of the largest herds of prize-winning holstein cattle in the state of Michigan, acres of farmland, and gardens which were used as therapy for the patients. You are permitted to drive into the grounds, although some areas are restricted.

Now we cross Eleventh street and hit a dirt road which is usually well-maintained. On both sides was once State Hospital farmland. The brick building you see is the power plant, which supplies generated power to the hospital. The buildings you see in back of the power plant are patient cottages.

The railroad track which we cross is now abandoned. It supplied coal to the power plant and supplies to the hospital.

We reach a stop at the Silver Lake road, and jog briefly to the right. Again, ahead of us and to the right and to the left is State Hospital land, now all abandoned from the farming projects and gardening rehabilitation fields for which it was once famous.

Ahead and to the left you'll see the junior high school. We're now entering an area which was known as the "Elm Flats." Turn left on Franke road.

Ahead on the left you see an assembly of business buildings, a shopping plaza. On your left once stood a building, only recently torn down, which was the home of the "Swamp Angels," and was called "Swamp House," a house of prostitution.

Now, on the right is the Brookside subdivision, which was built on low ground, and once presented a problem of drainage.

We now proceed on Franke road and head directly into the Oleson farm, and if you are fortunate, as we go over the hill, you will see a herd of several hundred buffalo for which Gerald Oleson, a Traverse City businessman, is famous. He has devoted a great deal of time and energy to creating the herd, which is the largest east of the Mississippi. He sells the meat in his grocery stores as well as donating large amounts for a huge college barbeque to the benefit of Northwestern Michigan College each spring.

The buffalo range on large acreage off to your right as you turn left back into Traverse City on U.S. 31. As we move back into Traverse City, we see how business has exerted its sprawling influence. Business places are mushrooming and condominiums are being constructed; many already completed.

Into Traverse City turn right on Fourteenth street (at the traffic light) and note how the city has crept, building by building, to the south.

Despite the growth and development, and increased traffic, the Traverse City area and the Grand Traverse region has remained a mecca for those who wish to get away from the hustle and the bustle of an environment to which man was never intended to acclimate.

We follow Fourteenth street and turn right on Rennie, designated many years ago as Blue Star highway. On the right is an early resort area. When this was the main highway north and south, motels welcomed visitors here with what we would consider bargain prices. At the top of Rennie Hill is a flat area. On the left will be the Traverse City County Club and golf course and, on the right, the old Traverse City circus grounds. It was here that Ringling Brothers and Barnum and Bailey set up their big tents. Here the first airport was created and here the first mail in the United States was flown in by glider. The mail came from Frankfort during the heyday of gliding fever.

Vista Manor subdivision occupies the old circus grounds, and what was once an aircraft landing area. On your right ahead Memorial Gardens cemetery, one of the newer cemeteries in the community.

We turn left now at a junction with South Airport road. South Airport road is one of the newer highways connecting the community on the east side of Boardman river with that on the west. It was the dream of Merle Lutz, for many years secretary of the Traverse City Chamber of Commerce, who felt that there should be an access through the swampland across the Boardman river.

Since the construction of this road a few years ago, the area has developed into an exclusive and beautiful residential section.

We reach the foot of a grade and we'll notice that commercial sites have been developed, but over the whole, there is a neatness; not the clutter of the average industrial site.

We pass the Wysong gravel processing plant and down into the valley. It might be worth your time to pull into Logan's Landing shopping center; there's an assembly of boutiques and shops, a beautiful restuarant on the banks of the Boardman river, and here you will also find a public park, made possible by a gift from the Wysong interests.

If you are fortunate, and almost any day you can be fortunate, you can see swans, mallard ducks, and assorted wildlife on the south end of the Boardman Lake.

The mainstream of the Boardman river was changed during the lumbering days to its present channel. The bridge over which you just passed has two metal tubes. These tubes are large enough to permit the passage of a compact car through their length. The amount of water flowing through the tubes river was sufficient to float countless thousands of logs. In the early days the channel was deflected, as you will see now just before you cross the rise in the road. There is a metal fence on each side as we cross the old and original channel of the Boardman river. The change was made to give a straight shot for logs, which were floated down from the plains country and the Brownbridge area.

We're cresting the rise in the highway now and coming to the Chamber of Commerce Industrial park. This was another Lutz dream and development and has proved a tremendous success by segregating industry from possible residential areas.

Now we're coming to the stoplight and will turn left on Barlow. The area through which we're passing was originally named Boonville and then Boontown. It was, at one time, the slum area of Traverse City. One man in the area

155

boasted that the only cost involved in his house was $3.00 for nails and $2.00 for tarpaper.

You will notice that the area through which we are driving is now a very respectable residential area and as you wander on the side streets, you will become more aware that there is no slum area in Traverse City.

On the left is the Glacier Dome, devoted to winter and summer sports, with refrigeration for hockey in season and out. In the short time it has been in existence it has come into considerable prominence.

We come to a stop street and cross. On the right (Barlow and Center), is a yellow-green house which was the home of old Joe Boon; and at a later date that, also, became a house of small-time ill-repute.

We now see that Barlow becomes a gravel street. Homes here started tiny and as owners had money they built onto them. It's now a quiet and pleasant residential area, extending on the right to Garfield avenue.

We will turn left at a yield sign on a paved street, Hannah avenue, and go to the next stop sign which is a short block. We are now passing the old railroad yards of the Chesapeake and Ohio, before that the Michigan Central railroad. Here trains came into the hub of Traverse City activity. It was from here that trains departed for all points south.

We are at Eighth street. Turn left and head toward our terminal. Directly on the right, now a vacant lot with the railroad tracks running through it, was the old Hopkins ice house which served the community prior to the days of electric refrigeration. It was torn down many years ago when the day of the ice house was no more.

Ahead of us is a stop signal. As nearly as can be determined, it was directly beneath this light that Boardman built the first house in Traverse City and constructed a pole bridge across the Boardman river.

Just across the modern bridge, on your left, you will see an assembly of buildings. This was the location of the Napoleon Automobile company. The plant produced the

"Big Six" and the "Chummy Four" automobiles and the Glidden truck. The plant closed in 1918.

Our next tour will pick up a few points of interest in the city of Traverse City, but we will wander afield to see, here and there a ghost town, a lone grave, or the site of a pioneer industry, now dead but once vital to the growth and development of the region.

THE APPROXIMATE DISTANCE OF TOUR TWO WAS SEVEN MILES.

TOUR NUMBER THREE

Tour number three will take us east out of Traverse City through a pleasant residential area, through a country that was once covered with virgin pine and hardwood. We will pass through ghost towns and living communities, but every inch of the modern highways is bordered by history. The shades of the pioneers are reflected at every turn in the road and every tumbled-down building which we may pass.

Once again, using the Chamber of Commerce as a starting point, we head south on Cass street past the Milliken store, past the former location of the general store of Prokop Kyselka. Again, we pass the city hall and the police headquarters and turn left on Washington street.

On the left again, the Bo-Gi Club, which was the site of the Grange Hall nearly a century ago. We pass Jail Hill, which was the original building site of the county jail and the current site of the county courthouse. The jail has long since been removed and a new structure has been put in its place.

The hill on which the buildings were constructed was

once a burial mound for the Indians, prehistoric. In excavating for the original structure, workmen uncovered copper artifacts and utensils, arrowheads and bones. There is no record of what became of these items. They were around for a short time; there was a minor cataloguing, but it is basically evident that the hill was the site of a prehistoric village.

Now we pass Boardman avenue, and in front of a little white house (427), we see a gnarled oak tree with a bronze plaque in front of it, designating it as an Indian trail marker tree. This has been accepted for some time, but the tree is obviously not a trail marker tree. We do not say this to have an argument with anybody; but the trail marker trees of the Indians were bent over to the ground, weighted down, and then grew up in the shape of a letter "N" and a tree never grows from the bottom, it only grows from the top.

This would have had to have been a very tall Indian who bent the tree. We have consulted with a number of authorities, and while it was a fine gesture on the part of the orgainzation which marked the tree, it was a case of mistaken authority. A little later we will pass an authentic trail-marker tree.

On the left as we near Wellington street, still continuing on Washington, we approach Hull House, one of the most elaborate houses in the city, even outdoing the Perry Hannah home. The ballroom on the third floor was spacious, the woodwork was gorgeous, as was the entire interior, but it has been converted, in recent years, to apartments. It was a gathering place for Traverse City society during its heyday, during the period of the Ovalwood Dish company which Mr. Hull owned.

The beautiful home directly across Wellington street, also built by the Hull family has been completely refurbished as it was during the lumbering days.

We are now going through an area of residential property which in most part, was built by businessmen of Traverse City. We reach Railroad avenue and literally "cross the tracks." Here we come to more modest homes which in the past decades have been redone until this neighborhood is one of the most delightful parts of Traverse City.

We come to a stop at Rose street and turn left two blocks to East Front street. Here we turn right (east) on U.S. 31 and toward the eastern limits of Traverse City.

Now, in the next four miles we'll be passing through an area that is somewhat unique in that it is almost all resort property and motels. It is called motel strip by many of the summer guests who come here, either for a day, a week, a month, or for the season.

On the left after crossing the Garfield avenue intersection, we come to a shopping complex, Campus Plaza. On the right is the old fairgrounds. If you'll observe closely over in the oaks across from the Kroger store, you'll see a bent oak tree in the shape of the letter "N." That is an authentic trail-marker tree, marking the trail from the north to Cadillac and points south.

A second tree located just outside the fairgrounds was recently destroyed and another near the airport on Garfield was also cut down.

You are now moving past, one after another, beautiful motel vacation accommodations. This type of building will continue for another four miles.

You pass the Munson Motor Inn on the left and the Pinecrest Motel on the right, and then where a Shell station is located just ahead of you, was the first motel in the Grand Traverse region. Many claims have been made about which was the first, but this was a series of little cabins owned by Ed Hallberg and operated for many, many years with an overnight rate of two dollars per couple.

Now we pass the Osteopathic Hospital, where once was a nine-hole golf course. The Osteopathic was originally located on Grandview parkway, as we mentioned in another tour, but it outgrew its headquarters.

We continue east on U.S. 31 headed for the village of Elk Rapids, past the large shopping center on the right, and for a short distance we pass a subdivision development where, fifty years ago, they were selling lots for twenty dollars and giving them away as prizes at movie theaters. It didn't come into its own until 20 to 30 years ago and now it is built solid with pleasant homes.

Ahead of us is a slight curve in the road. It was here on the left that the old Mitchell Mill was located. This settlement was then known as East Bay. The old boarding house for the Mitchell Mill is now Shields restuarant, plus another house which was torn down.

We cross Mitchell creek, named for the Mitchell family. Indian Trails resort, which took over from the mill operation on the creek, was also here and operated for some time quite successfully.

We pass the Traverse City state park on the right. Here you may still see a number of specimens of virgin timber but we still are touring motel area.

Now we pass a series of motels and courts on the left and right, very close together. Then, on the left is a public boat launching site. It was here that the old O-at-ka Beach Resort was located. It was a dance and fun spot which, in its day was both bad and good, having a reputation which you could take either way.

And then, little yellow cabins . . . Baker's Acres. It was here that a sawmill operated for many years before the turn of the century.

Now we come to a fork in the road and we keep to the right. This was the old U.S. 31 many years ago. The new pavement around the edge of East Bay by-passed the old highway.

The water you see to your left is the east arm of Grand Traverse Bay. We come to a railroad track which has a stop sign . . . it does mean stop. This is just one of the things that you may pass lightly, but it was here that, several years ago, an automobile containing seven people was struck by the train and all but one of them was killed. At that time the sheriff's department and the county board of supervisors decided that it should be a stop zone.

Now the road forks again, and we go to the left. The right fork takes you up through plains country and the Holiday Hills ski resort. We are still on the old highway. The homes you see, many of them, have been constructed

161

during the past ten to fifteen years. This was always a very scenic road and very popular before the construction of the new highway. Now you see a glimpse here and there of the new road and we'll pass in a few moments on the right the excavation where the earth was removed to fill the edge of the beach and make room for the new highway.

We are now approaching the village of Acme, a pleasant resort village today, originally named Whitewater. It was founded when the Hoxie family built a woolen mill and there was an immediate influx of employees. It was never a lumbering town, despite the fact that it had a couple of mills.

The postoffice was removed at one time and the village deteriorated for a while. It seemed as though Acme would become another ghost town. But the beautiful beach and the miles and miles of blue water brought an influx of residents again, and the postoffice was re-established and the town once again came to life.

Now in the heart of the village of Acme, we turn right on M-72. If this road were to continue to our left, or across the bay, it would come out where Greilickville is now located and cross in front of the Homeopathic hospital, which we mentioned in another tour.

We will now pass through rolling farm country, vast acres which were at one time noted for potato production. We will also pass through one or two ghost towns.

For the next few miles relax and enjoy the countryside, the beautiful golf course, the Sand Trap on the left, and then the rolling hills with fruit farms, general agriculture, dairy farms, and just good American residential area.

We might point out as we drive along this area that there is and has been of recent times, an oil strike. A village which we will approach very soon, Williamsburg, was demoralized when a gas leak forced almost every resident out of the village. The water became contaminated because of oil and gas, and until the well could be plugged, people for weeks, and in some cases months, were forced to remain away from their homes.

Ahead now is a railroad crossing and you've reached

the little town of Bates, which was once a potato shipping center. There is nothing here now in the way of business, but at one time it was a bustling village named after the Thomas T. Bates family of Traverse City. The stone building you see on the right was a home for the infirm. A postoffice was established here in 1891 and closed in 1931. One of the largest potato warehouses in the area was located on the right at the crossing.

We move on now through still rolling farmland with many newly planted orchards, and approach the village of Williamsburg, which has been moved twice as the highway was moved. On the third location of the highway, Williamsburg decided to stay where it is, on the left of the main thoroughfare.

It will be worth your while to drive down to the old village as well as the new. We are going to turn right at the "Elk Lake road" sign and go through the old village.

The church which we see ahead on the left was constructed over 100 years ago by voluntary labor. It is a Methodist church, refurbished recently.

Turn left in front of the ancient church, and proceed down a grade and across a stream. Watch closely and you will see on your right the site of the old Eation and Stites Mill.

The old mill in this location took its power from the creek which we have just crossed. If you look closely you will see a garage with the sign "Millbrook." Now you have a chance to catch a glimpse of some of the old mill buildings. It is privately owned now and not open to tours, but it still has the millpond, and the entire mill assembly has been kept as it was in the days of the pioneers.

Now we reach the end of the road and turn left. The old boarding house is a brick building on your right after you make your left turn. Another boarding house has been torn down.

Directly on your left is a vacant lot on which stood the general store. Then we pass a building which is the old town hall. Now, back to the main highway just short of Buttermilk Corners. Directly ahead of us and under a railway

163

overpass was the creamery where they churned butter and sold buttermilk, hence the name "Buttermilk Corners."

We'll head out on the new highway driving east. If we continued on this road, we would either fork to the left and go through Rapid City or we could curve to the right and go through Kalkaska. However, we are going to the ghost village of Mable.

Mable Bates was a member of the pioneer Bates family of Traverse City, and the village was named in honor of her. It had, at one time, a store with a beautiful flowing well, which shot water in the air higher than a two-story building. Mable was a trading center for the potato growers who had found the climate and the land conducive to the production of the crop.

Now that we have given you a little of the background of the tiny village which doesn't exist, we will move on to view the remains.

Cross the railroad track and go down a grade. On the right is an inconspicuous highway, Watson road. Turn here. Slow and across the creek ahead. At the top of the rise you are at the site of the old village of Mable. On your left you can still see the great flow of water coming from the old well.

Mable is only a memory now, but when it was first established and given a postoffice, it was the hub of community business. The postoffice closed in 1918. The geographical location of the village was between section 35 and two, range nine west for both descriptions.

Back again to the main highway and turn right. Around a long curve and over a ridge and you are in Kalkaska county. Vanished without a trace is the village of Barker Creek, which was located on the creek of that name in the little valley just ahead.

Barker Creek received its postoffice in 1874 and was a better-than-average town for many years. Postal service was discontinued in 1930. Beyond the village site and on the right is the remains of the old church cemetery. It is an interesting place to explore.

Only a short distance more, on your right, is a scenic

turn-out and it is here we retrace our steps to the village of Williamsburg, back over highway 72 westward.

After passing Watson road on our left, we once again cross the rails and turn to the right onto "Old 72." Once again, turn right on the Williamsburg road and head for Elk Rapids.

Elk Rapids was founded in 1865 when Henry Noble organized a firm with a partner named Dexter.

Three years after the founding of the Dexter and Noble enterprise, the first pig iron in the history of American enterprise was shipped out of New York for European markets. It was poured in Elk Rapids.

We will visit the sight of the old iron works, where the plant was located at the edge of a great sand dune, long since gone. At one time the sand dune drifted in over the Dexter and Noble boarding house. The structure was later excavated and torn down. We will see the Island House and drive the length of the main street, which is through the heart of a beautiful and still growing village.

We drive the Williamsburg road to Elk Rapids, along a part of the Chain-of-Lakes. It was through this chain of lakes that Dexter and Noble operated a score of boats hauling timber and passengers. We are approaching an intersection, a stop street. We turn right and are back on U.S. 31 north and on the southern outskirts of Elk Rapids.

Taking a pattern from the Traverse City industrial area, Elk Rapids too has set aside industrial land as you see on your right (across from the Cherry Bucket restuarant) where the road bypasses the village proper.

We will tour the village of Kewadin and will return to the main street of the village of Elk Rapids. But for now we give heed to this industrial complex which, to the resident of a big city, might look rather wan and puny.

On the right now you see the backwater from the old Dexter and Noble dam, see where the stumps are left standing when the trees were cut.

We will turn right at the flasher. The old sand dune was on the left, and it was there that part of the iron foundry was located. On the right you will see the Elk River Inn and motel complex and in back of that there is a monument on a pile of slag. Here you may see a plaque dedicated to the iron company and its industrial pioneering. Stop and read it.

This part of Elk Rapids is called East Elk Rapids: modest homes and pleasant surrounding.

Now we are leaving East Elk Rapids and are on old highway 31 heading for the Indian village of Kewadin. A rather interesting note is that the houses across the way from the golf course which we are passing suffered many broken windows from stray golf balls.

You will notice the unpretentious but lovely homes that line the lakeshore in this drive to the Indian community of Kewadin.

Now we enter the village of Kewadin. You pass a cemetery on your left, but this is not the old Indian cemetery.

On through the village and we pass the Indian church on the left, and back of the church is the Kewadin Indian cemetery. The church is a pleasant little white building, and in back you'll see the crosses in the cemetery where the Indians have been buried for over a century.

It is here that the old medicine man Aish-Qua-Gwa-Naba is buried. His grave is unmarked, but someplace beneath the flowers and sod is old medicine man Aish-Qua-Gwa-Naba. He was buried with a rope with a hook on the end of it, so that, if he got into the great city in the sky and he was unable to scale the wall, he could throw the hook over the edge of it and climb up. He was also buried with some of the scalps which he treasured highly.

You will do well to turn in at the little church, park your car, and look at the little burial ground.

We now leave the cemetery and follow the highway east and north. We're going to stop briefly at the Hugh Gray cairn.

We'll turn left at the first opportunity on a blacktop road which is, again, old 31, now called Chippewa Trail. The cairn which you will be approaching on your right was erected in honor of the founder and first president of the West Michigan Tourist and Resort Association and is built from boulders contributed from every county in the state. It is a very outstanding monument.

We wind back over the same highway on which we came and we will soon turn sharply to the right; you pass a cement block house on your left, and just a short distance past this, take a sharp turn to your right on a blacktop road to go past the old Indian village. The Indian settlement will be on the left, a rather unattractive collection of shacks . . . each one a home to somebody.

Turn left at the next stop street, then right and back onto the main highway to Elk Rapids and Traverse City.

We are once again approaching the outskirts of East Elk Rapids. We will cross 31 (new 31) at a flasher and proceed past the old Dexter and Noble holdings. The dam which they constructed will be visible on your right and then down through the main part of the village of Elk Rapids.

We want to call your particular attention to the island in the middle of the river. It is now a library, but was once the home of Mr. Noble, who co-founded the industrial empire which is Elk Rapids.

Now we see the new breakwater and quiet water harbor. Off to your far right is the Island House, early home of Mr. Noble, which was later presented to the village and is now a public library. It can be reached by a footpath or by the road.

Turn to the right and you are on the main street of Elk Rapids.

If you have time to attend a cinema, there is a very unusual theater on your left. Decorated by a nationally and internationally know artist, the interior of the theater is unique and the shows which they present are just as unique as the decor.

On the right is a public park; now you can see more easily the boardwalk which goes across to the Island House. Note also the old town hall to the left and on the right further down, a school bell from the century old school, which was razed some years ago.

Now we come to a sharp turn to the left, the end of the street, and then a right turn.

On your right we will pass the site of the old cement plant which was one of the pioneer industries of Elk Rapids. Feel free to stop your car and wander among the old remains. A narrow guage railroad ran from the cement plant to an area about three miles south of the city. Here marl, used to manufacture cement, was loaded on the cars. This plant, established so long ago, moved to Petosky in 1911, and is still operating there today.

You will notice as you proceed along this road, several of the dated motels, little cabins, and cottages. These early resort accommodations were the standby of the traveler a short memory ago.

We are approaching new 31, and once again we'll be wandering through heavy fruit growing country: apples, pears, cherries, and general farming land. Come to a stop street: new 31. Straight across is a "Wanigan Building Service." We have often wondered why they would call it the Wanigan service because a wanigan was a floating boarding house which followed the lumbering drives on the rivers and lakes and contained facilities for feeding the crew.

Incidentally, as we drive through this country, we can be aware that the narrow guage railway serving the cement plant went to the right of us on this modern highway. It might be interesting to know that a twelve hour day in the cement plant drew a wage of $1.98 for heavy work such as loading clay, filling hoppers and so forth. Skilled workers got just a little more. They went to work at 6:00 in the morning and worked until 6:00 in the evening.

The clay used in the manufacture of cement was taken from Petobego Swamp. You will see the sign for the swamp on your left. Park your car, if you wish, and take a closer look.

We go down a little dip in the road and a turn to the right after we cross Petobego creek, which drains Petobego Swamp.

Once again we're moving along the highway through farmland. We come to a farm complex where the barn is on the left and the housing facility is on the right, a light green assembly. After we pass through this "Morrison community" (which is what this is called), we will come to the grave of the first white child to die and be buried in this region.

Come to a blacktop road to your right and then jog directly left onto a little dirt trail. Don't follow the road to

Grand Traverse Bay, but turn immediately left on the dirt road, which is a temporary access to the grave.

The child's name was William Leith, and you'll notice the monument under the great white pine. He died in 1859 at the age of two years. The little marble tombstone that you see was brought into the area from Ohio by oxcart and then by overland trail. The parents came here to take part in the lumbering operation and the father was employed at a nearby mill at the time of the child's death.

We now move ahead onto highway 31 at the little village of Yuba, at one time a very prosperous town with a postoffice, mill, boarding house, store, and homes. The only thing left now in Yuba is the church and the Trading Post store.

We're now on our way back to Traverse City. Sit back in your seat and just enjoy the rolling land. You man catch an occasional view of Grand Traverse Bay. And, as we move farther on past the village of Acme, we see the skyline of Traverse City.

Anon, we'll be back home at the Chamber of Commerce building from which we started.

THE DISTANCE COVERED IN THE TOUR WHICH WE HAVE JUST COMPLETED, TOUR NUMBER THREE, WAS JUST UNDER SIXTY MILES.

TOUR NUMBER FOUR

Tour number four will take us on a drive through one of the most pleasant areas in the Grand Traverse region. It is the Old Mission Peninsula, jutting into Grand Traverse Bay and dividing it into its east and west parts.

We leave the Chamber of Commerce and head east on the boulevard. Follow Front street to Peninsula drive; that will be the fork in the road at a store called the Blue Goat ('75).

Take the left hand fork, at the stop sign turn left. Coming to a "Y" in the road, take the right hand highway, which is called, by the natives of the region, Center road. It follows the ridge of the Peninsula and offers many pleasant views. We will be driving through intensive fruit farming areas: apples, peaches and both sweet and tart cherries. In fact, the Peninsula is the most concentrated cherry-growing area in the United States.

Now, as you reach a crest of a hill, you will see both east and west arms of Grand Traverse Bay. On the left you will notice Marion Island which has been acquired by the public through the generosity of an Ann Arbor philanthropist, Eugene Power, to be used as a county recreational area.

The Peninsula is about a mile in width at its narrowest point and up to four miles at it widest point. It was on the Peninsula that the first cherry festival, at that time called the Blossom Festival, was held.

The blessing of the Blossoms in the spring of the year was a traditional event in years gone by, and blossom time is one of the most beautiful times of the year for this tour. It is then the orchards are white or, perhaps you prefer the harvest season when they have taken on the bloom of red from the ripening fruit.

For a considerable distance, the highway follows the east shore of the bay: that is the west shore of the east arm.

On your left, at approximately five miles, you will see a small county picnic area among shaded trees. Here are rustic restroom facilities.

Past the picnic area you will see a turn to the right. It might be an interesting drive; it goes around what is commonly called Bluff Road, where there is a sudden rise in the terrain and the road follows a very scenic shoreline. During the spring breakup, it is not uncommon for ice to be driven in from the force of the wind and completely close this road.

We will continue on Center road. Around a curve and up another grade. We are now approaching the very dense cherry producing area of the Peninsula. On the right you will see a processing plant where the cherries are brined for marischino cherries, and where the producers of the area concentrate during the harvest season.

This particular road was not used by the settlers who first came here; the pioneer road was on the west shore on what is now Peninsula drive, and this road, in terms of years, is relatively new. Perhaps the first trail through here was in 1870 or 75.

Now on your left, after driving down a small grade (just past Island View road), you will see a small cemetery. It might be worth your while to stop just a few moments to wander through and see the names and graves of the pioneers of Old Mission Peninsula; Ross, Emory, and so forth. It was here that a number of Indian graves were made when the remains were transported from the Old Mission Point area to a new burial grounds. These graves will be in the right hand corner of the cemetery, marked mostly by stakes because identification was impossible.

It was here that Frank and Ida Kroupa, pioneers, are buried, and one plot of eight graves is marked with little white crosses to indicate the religious faith.

Leaving the little cemetery, we move on through the fertile farmland, heading for the end of the Old Mission Peninsula.

Now as we reach a fork in the road, that is St. Joseph's Catholic church on the right. Take the right hand fork and note the old schoolhouse on the left hand road. It has been long since abandoned as a school, and revamped into a residence. The public schools on the Peninsula, most of them the one-room variety, were closed and in their place a modern, consolidated school was built on Island View road.

We now reach the tiny village of Mapleton. It is no longer a village. There is a small store to the right and a farm store on the left, all that is left of the village which was once a busy and growing community with a postoffice. It is here that the community fire department is located.

Still following the winding road which maintains a position on the top of the ridge, we are approaching another fork in the road. Smoky Hollow road goes down through a valley to the right, through rich farming country. Keep left.

We are now approaching the Old Mission Peninsula village called, of course, Old Mission.

Now and again you will catch a glimpse of the bay on either side of the highway as the road crests a hill here and there. There is the sign! Old Mission is to the right and we will turn sharply. Follow this road for about a mile to an intersection and turn left.

Old Mission village was founded in 1839 when Reverend Peter Dougherty came as a missionary to the Indian.

It was here that Reverend Dougherty built a bark shack in 1839. Later it was rebuilt into a modern home which is still standing. Midway into town and on your right you will see the Old Mission Center. This is a replica of the old church which Rev. Dougherty constructed to serve the Indians. It is believed to be exact in every detail, even to the bell in the tower. This building is open to the public. Stop here and spend a few moments.

Now, on your right, is an open field and it was here that the Indian settlement was located when Rev. Mr. Dougherty arrived. If you look carefully you will see a maple tree off to your right on the shore of the bay. Beside it (1975) is the dead stump of a second maple tree. These two trees were twigs when they were planted in front of the little bark shack of a squaw. It was her way of landscaping. Those trees were set over a century ago.

Now on your left, just a few hundred feet ahead, you will see a white house; a frame building, and in front of it a granite rock with a plaque. The message on the bronze plaque states: "The Old Mission House. Here Rev. Peter Dougherty and his wife, Maria Higgins, conducted their Indian mission, built in 1842, the first frame house in the Grand Traverse region. Tablet placed by M.H. Dougherty and Anna Dougherty Howard, aided by Job Winslow Chapter, Daughters of the American Revolution, 1927." The home is still in fairly good condition, although in recent years it has not been occupied.

We move on down the road to the village of Old Mission proper. This was once a very important town in the transportation business. Cherries, when they were first brought into the region, apples, potatoes, were raised by the countless thousands of bushels and shipped from the harbor here.

The dock area has since been donated to the village and it is now a park. We will turn around at the harbor and head back through Old Mission. Watch for a sign and turn right to Old Mission lighthouse.

Follow the blacktop on now to the point of the Peninsula, where the first lighthouse in the region was erected to protect shipping from the great boulders at the point.

Very little resort settlement here as we cruise along the

west shore of the Peninsula. You are heading toward the tip of the Peninsula.

As you drive along this sparsely settled road, it's hard to believe that just beyond that little ridge of trees lies the west arm of Grand Traverse Bay.

Round the curve, you come to a wide spot in the road, a scenic turn-out. On your right as you face the water, you'll see (1975) two or three little trees sticking out of the water. They are growing on what is left of a tiny island that was at one time the bane of sailing vessels and later the steamers. You will notice the white water; the area is infested with boulders and is a favorite bass fishing spot. Continue north and on your left is a public park and a monument. We are going to be stopping here for a moment.

This monument is a memorial to the veterans of World Wars I and II. You are now parked almost exactly on the 45th parallel. As you are parked, you are within a few rods of being halfway between the equator and the North Pole. This line runs from the Old Mission across the bay, goes through just north of Suttons Bay, and out at Bass Lake at the corner of Highways 204 and M-22.

Now we turn left on a short gravel road and see the sign that says "You are now standing on the 45th parallel." You'll also note by the sign that the lighthouse in front of you was built in 1870.

We reverse our direction and go back over a portion of the highway we have already covered. We will leave it at Mapleton, and in doing so, we will soon be following the route followed by the pioneers when they wanted to go to Traverse City or to points south. Note how the pioneer trail so closely followed the shore. It was on this, the Chippewa level, that travel was the easiest.

Keep directly ahead. Over the grade, as we move along Center road, on a clear day the views on this road are beautiful, reminding one of the Black Hills of South Dakota or even the approaches to the Ozarks.

It might be a good idea to slow up a bit; the whole drive is not going to take you too long. Breathe deeply of the fresh pure air. Enjoy every curve of this beautiful winding highway.

Now as you approach the village of Mapleton, you'll pass the fire department. On past the little country store and the farm implement store. Now take a sharp downhill turn to the right.

You are now headed directly into the west arm of the bay. Again you will get a glimpse of the bright blue water. Be cautious, this is a rather busy intersection ahead, especially during the summer months.

On the left as you round the curve you will see a recreation area where they have horse shows, and for many years it has been a spot where the young folks have gathered for competitive sports.

Stop and turn left at the village of Bowers Harbor. There is a bronze plaque on a boulder which points out that it is here that S.E. Wait taught the first school in the Grand Traverse area. It was aboard the schooner *Madeline* anchored out in the bay directly west of the village.

It was at this location, also that a man named Bower, with his family, sought refuge fron the dictatorship of King Ben Strang on Beaver Island. On the right through the foilage you can see Marion Island. A few years ago it was a heavily forested, virgin timber island, but it was logged off by an industrial firm in Traverse City. Only recently it was acquired as a recreational area.

Just to the north of the big island there is a tiny strip of land called Bassett Island. Dick Bassett settled there long before the turn of the century and operated a fishing business. He was a hermit and a veteran of the Civil War and operated a fish store on East Front street in Traverse City.

Later the little island became a resort and a large dance hall was constructed. Passenger service was rendered each weekday from Traverse City to the island and back. Even today, if you walk over the island, you will see remains of the old dance hall, piled in rotting heaps among the trees. And some of old Dick Bassett's apple trees are still growing and bearing fruit.

Now after winding through a brush-lined road, we come to the beginning of the heavily populated section of the west bay road. Some of the most beautiful homes in the region are located along this highway. In the distance on the right you can see the shoreline of Traverse City.

We're back again, after a drive through one of the most historic areas in the Grand Traverse region, where the first white settler came, where missionaries first sought to bring their beliefs to the Indians. And, it was on the Peninsula that the first settlement was directed.

TOUR NUMBER FOUR HAS COVERED
APPROXIMATELY 60 MILES AND HAS
TAKEN ABOUT TWO HOURS.

TOUR NUMBER FIVE

Tour number five is undoubtedly one of the most colorful in the Grand Traverse area. It takes us north the length of the little finger of the mitten-shaped state of Michigan. The highway, M-22, can be a continuous route for the complete tour north along the east shore of the Peninsula and back on the west shore. Once again, we'll be driving through farmlands, fruit producing communities, and some of the finest resort and summer guest areas in the Middle West.

Leaving the Chamber of Commerce, we head north and west on Grandview Parkway, past Clinch Park, which was once the site of the "Big Mill," past the site of the former Morgan canning plant, pioneers in the cherry processing business, and on to the intersection of M-72 at the village of Greilickville, which is really an urban part of Traverse City.

On the side of the hill, back of the West Bay Shopping Center to your left, was the site of the first hospital in the Grand Traverse Bay region. It was homeopathic and operated for several years before it was destroyed by fire.

We move north on highway M-22 through the once

prosperous and bustling village. Originally this village was called Norrisville in honor of the family which pioneered in the lumbering and gristmill business on the little creek which we will soon cross.

The Norris mill was located on the right hand side as we cross the bridge over Cedar creek. The dam is still in place and in the basement of the little Spanish-style house is complete generating equipment for power.

We are now approaching, on the left, a high bank separating Cedar lake from Grand Traverse bay. The clay of this bank was used in a brick manufactory at the turn of the century and provided white brick for the construction of the State Hospital buildings of that era as well as such buildings as the Hannah-Lay Mercantile and the Masonic buildings in Traverse City.

On the left you will see a sign, "Pathfinder School." Here has been established a pioneer study center at which you may hear an audio-visual presentation on the lives of the pioneers of the Grand Traverse region. It is open to the public during the summer months only.

Now, for about twelve or fifteen miles, you will follow the left shore of Grand Traverse bay. It is indeed a scenic wonderland, whether it is summer, spring, autumn or winter; one of the most perfect drives in the region. At about fifteen miles on your trip around the little finger, you will approach the quiet village of Suttons Bay.

This town was originally founded by a Catholic priest in 1871, with a dream of building a school and college in a complete Catholic settlement. It was then called Pleasantville City. Later it was renamed, after the failure of the religious development, in honor of Captain H.C. Sutton. It was called Suttonsburg at that time. Later the "burg" was dropped and it is today Suttons Bay.

Through Suttons Bay, past the intersection of highway M-204, we continue north past a fruit packing plant and, once again, at a pleasant little turnout on the right hand side just a short distance beyond Suttons Bay, we cross the 45th parallel, again we are halfway between the Equator and the North Pole. You are now in a direct line equatorially with the Old Mission Peninsula lighthouse, which we visited on an earlier tour.

Now around the curve and across the railroad tracks, which was once the main connecting link between the tip of the peninsula, Traverse City, and points south.

We are now about ten miles from the village of Northport. You notice as you cross the railroad track, there is a small accommodations place with a large sign which says "45th parallel."

The road we are following is almost completely on the old Indian footpath of the earlier days, later the dirt road which the pioneers used.

Now up a grade, and we are approaching the Indian village of Peshawbestown, named after an early chieftan, Peshawbe. The village is not a reservation, strictly speaking, but is a cluster of native homes on property primarily owned by the public.

At the edge of the village we approach the Catholic church, and the quaint and quiet well-kept cemetery behind the church. You will do well to stop here just for a few moments, and walk through the quietness of the cemetery. Note, as you stroll, the great number of Indian names, Peshawbe, Kingbird, and so on and on.

In back, in the right hand corner, observe two large cedar trees growing side by side. They are the only monument that a mother could afford when her twin children died during an epidemic. Also note that almost all of the markers are wooden crosses, indicative of lack of affluence on the part of the native people.

A monument in front of the Catholic church was erected by the Masonic order and the bronze plaque states that the Chippewa tribe settled here in 1845. That was when the church at Old Mission was moved across the bay and was settled on Omena bay. The Catholics settled in this particular area and, a short distance ahead, in the village of Omena, the protestant people settled.

And now we once again cross the railroad track and the north boundary of the village.

On the left now we see the Villa Marquette, which is a

retreat for Catholic priests of the Jesuit order. Then, into the village of Omena. It was here that Reverend Peter Dougherty brought his church when he left Old Mission. The word "omena" in the Ottawa language means "so be it."

Around a bend, past the postoffice and store, and on the right you see the original church which Reverend Dougherty built. The bell in the steeple is made from copper pennies collected from the native people. Back of the church is a small cemetery and it is here that Chief Agosa is buried. He was an early chieftan of the tribe and his descendants still live in the area.

On now, past the church, toward the village of Northport. The area through which we are now driving is once again fruit producing, a fertile light loam.

At the southern edge of the village of Northport, follow highway 201. We will return on M-22 after a visit to some of the interesting points beyond.

Follow the highway signs through the village of Northport proper. Here you will find numerous places to shop and browse, quaint little art shops and antique stores. The village of Northport was settled in 1849, when Reverend George Smith arrived. He came to work with the Indians of the Grand Traverse region, and remained throughout his lifetime.

The Indians of this village were at that time headed by Chief Waukazoo, and the village was first named after this band of Indians and called Waukazooville. Even today one of the streets is Waukazoo street.

After shopping around at the village, perhaps having lunch at one of the little eating places, we move on north, following highway M-201. When highway 201 ends, go straight on through the intersection. Do not turn to the right, because we are going to visit Peterson Park and see one of the loveliest views in the Grand Traverse region.

Turn left at the end of the road, after coming to a complete stop. Once again we're driving through fertile fruit growing land.

At a sharp bend to the left, be alert. You are now about to turn right and drive directly into Peterson Park.

It was here at Peterson Park that a band of pagan Indians once lived. Their burial ground on the other side of the woods to the right of the park has been bulldozed over to make way for a modern housing development, and the score or more of graves have been destroyed. Park your car in the space available and walk to the fence.

On a clear day you can see the Fox Islands (North and South) in the distance. Even on a hazy, foggy day, they loom through the mist. Perhaps a freighter is passing, for you are looking directly onto one of the main shipping lanes of Lake Michigan. There is a stairway leading down to the beach, where you may find Petoskey stones, even an agate; in addition to that the walk will certainly be good for you.

To your left in the park are facilities. There is ample picnic space and permanent stoves for the convenience of guests. This park was made available to the public by Anne Peterson Raymond in memory of Hans Peterson. It is the property of Leelanau township.

After resting and admiring the view across the great lake, we return to Northport, retracing our trail and picking up M-22 at the southern edge of the village. Be alert as you go back out onto M-22. Turn sharp; watch for traffic.

You are now headed for the village of Leland. This road, like the northbound section of M-22, was once a trail used by the natives; and there was a considerable settlement of Indian people along the way.

About four miles along your trip since leaving Northport, you will see an Indian church of the Methodist faith. On these grounds for many years, the Indian people have held camp meetings.

You are now five miles south of Northport, and on your left you will see a little tavern, which has become famous for its outstanding food and friendly atmosphere. If you didn't take time out for a bite of lunch before, you can do no better than to stop here.

Now into the little village of Leland, famous throughout the northland as a fishing village. Here commercial fishermen have operated since the settlement was first started in 1848.

Park your car and walk down through the little shorefront area called "Fishtown." Here you can buy the famous Leland smoked fish, or shop in one of the quaint stores in the rickety buildings which border the water. Or perhaps you may want to shop in the colonial type buildings on the main street.

Leland is a summer town, with a winter population of a few people. Accommodations during the summer season are almost impossible to find unless reservations are made in advance. Now that you have had a short stroll and a shopping trip through Leland, we head on south on M-22. Two miles south of the village, turn left on the intersection of M-204. You are now heading back towards Traverse City and have left M-22.

Lake Leelanau, four miles ahead, was founded in 1867, when there was talk of an oil boom in the community. It was first called "The Narrows" because of the little river which connects the two sections of Lake Leelanau. It was later named "Provemont," and still later the name was changed to Lake Leelanau.

At this point, after crossing the narrows on the modern bridge, you can either turn right and follow highway 641 to your point of beginning in Traverse City, or you can continue on M-204 to Suttons Bay. On highway 641 you will be following the east shore of south Lake Leelanau, and you'll be passing through a considerable amount of farmland as well as resort property. You will enter Traverse City on Cherry Bend road and turn right on M-22. You are soon back in Traverse City at your point of beginning.

THIS TOUR WAS APPROXIMATELY 75 MILES.

UNGUIDED TOURS IN THE GRAND TRAVERSE BAY AREA AND ADDITIONAL POINTS OF INTEREST YOU SHOULD VISIT

The entire area around the Little Finger Peninsula, Old Mission Peninsula, and the vast area inland, is dotted with interesting historical places.

No resident or guest of the area should fail to visit the Beulah-Benzonia community. A part of the old college still stands on the Benzonia hill which overlooks the pretty village of Beulah.

A drive to Frankfort will take you past the "dream river" where a group of engineers and residents tried to create a channel between Crystal Lake and the Frankfort harbor. One boat made the trip through the new outlet and the dream brought an awakening to the impossibility of the plan.

Frankfort is a harbor town. Car ferries of the Ann Arbor Railroad operate out of its deep water.

Lake Ann, the village which wouldn't die, is another place with a fighting history. Three times it burned and three times it refused to die. It is located on the shores of a lake by the same name and is in Benzie county.

Don't miss a short visit to the once big town of Sherman. At one time this ghost town was the county seat of Wexford county. It boasted plans for a brilliant future. But, adversity struck and the county seat was moved to Cadillac. Sherman is still there on M-37 south . . . only a shadow of its early self.

Fife Lake and Walton Junction east of Kingsley are two villages with reputations. They, at one time, were known as the "fightingest towns in the north" and each had scars to prove it. Walton Junction is no longer a town . . . just a pleasant turn-off . . . and Fife Lake still exists although there are no dreams of big cityhood.

The lake area south and east of Traverse City is also a must for a quiet drive. The pleasant roads through what once was dense pine and hardwood forest enables one to almost relive the turbulent days of the lumberjack and the steam sawmill.

Interlochen, just south and a bit west of Traverse City, is a once-in-a-lifetime treat for the whole family. When we say "Interlochen" we mean the National Music Camp near that village. Here the musical great and the performing artists of the nation congregate each summer to work, study, teach, and relax.

In any direction out of Traverse City you will drive the trails and footpaths of the Indian people and the pioneer residents. The area is so replete with lore and historical interest that you will come back again and again. You'll have to because you just can't cover it all in a single exploration.

THINGS YOU SHOULD KNOW ABOUT THE GRAND TRAVERSE BAY AREA

Many of these "firsts" were first published in the book *100 Years From the Old Mission*. Later, because school children were using the facts as a guide for regional history study, they were repeated in a subsequent book *Vinegar Pie*.

Again we learn that high school students as well as lower grades have used the text in their research for local history papers. With some additions, we again present it because we are so deeply interested in the accurate preservation of our area heritage.

. . .

The first white settlers in the Grand Traverse bay area were Rev. Dougherty and John Fleming. They arrived at Old Mission in 1839 and opened a mission for the Indians. Later Rev. Dougherty moved to Omena (New Mission) and continued his ministry.

The first frame building was erected at Old Mission by Rev. Dougherty and is still standing. For many years it was used as school, chapel and residence.

. . .

The first public school in the Grand Traverse bay area was a log building located near the Boardman river between Boardman avenue and Wellington street. The building was an old stable renovated for the few students.

. . .

The first school teacher was Miss Helen Goodale. She lived at the Hannah, Lay and Company boarding house and walked to her school each morning.

. . .

The first mail service in the region was in 1849 when two letters and a magazine were delivered by John Campbell. Later a semi-regular mail service was established, dependent on Indian carriers between Traverse City and Manistee. Jake Ta-pa-sa delivered the first mail north.

. . .

The first steam boat to enter Grand Traverse bay was the *Michigan*. The date was April 14, 1851.

. . .

The first postoffice in the area was at Old Mission (Grand Traverse). The postmaster was W.R. Stone and he kept the mail in a wooden raisin box nailed to the kitchen wall.

. . .

The first wedding in the community was in 1842 when Ansel Salisbury came across the lake from Wisconsin to marry Olive Dame.

. . .

The first white child to be born in the region was Henry Miller. The baby was born to Mr. and Mrs. Lewis Miller in 1846.

Horace Boardman and Michael Gay were the first white people to settle in the Traverse City area. They arrived in 1847 aboard a sailing ship and started lumbering operations where the city now stands.

. . .

The first church constructed in the Grand Traverse bay area was in 1842. It was erected at Old Mission and a replica has been built and is open to the public.

. . .

The first civic organization of record in the area was "The Mutual Admiration Society." There is no exact date of its organization but it continued for several years.

. . .

The first store or "mercantile business" was opened by Hannah, Lay and Company. The store was located on the north side of Boardman river and on the east side of Union street.

. . .

The first house in Traverse City was built at the north end of Boardman lake about where Boardman avenue and East Eighth street intersect. It was a log blockhouse, built as a sort of fortress against possible Indian attack. Remember, no one knew too much about the region at that early date or the possible threat from hostile natives.

. . .

The first bridge across the Boardman river was at the present location of the East Eighth street bridge. It was built of poles and provided a crossing for the residents of the "blockhouse." Date, 1847.

. . .

Hannah, Lay and Company erected the first steam sawmill in Traverse City. It was built on a site formerly occupied by the Morgan-McCool canning firm and where Clinch Park is now located.

187

James Lee and Ann Dakin were married in the first such ceremony performed within the village of Traverse City. It was in 1853.

. . .

Josephine Gay was the first white child born in the village of Traverse City. She was born to Mr. and Mrs. Michael Gay. Her birthday was May 15, 1849.

. . .

The Grand Traverse county courthouse (1975) is built on an ancient Indain mound. No record of the artifacts removed was ever kept.

. . .

There is an authentic Indian trail tree at the old county fairgrounds across from Campus Plaza Shopping Center.

. . .

The first Sunday school in Traverse City was organized in 1853.

. . .

There was once a city dump where the United States postoffice building now stands. Another village dump was near the beach at Clinch Park and, as late as 1930, it was common to see local marksmen shooting rats there during their lunch breaks.

. . .

Where Grandview parkway is located, and north of Boardman avenue, there was once an Indian campground. This was especially popular in the late summer months when the natives arrived in canoes and dugout boats to hunt and to pick wild berries.

. . .

The first opera house in Traverse City was built in the 100 block, East Front Street. The City Opera House still stands as an historical monument. It is owned by William Votruba and still has its ancient stage, box seats, and dance floor.

THE GIRLS

They were as much a part of the lumbering era as the river dog and the shingle mill. They were not the girls who milked the family cow, prepared a Sunday supper, or taught in the Sunday school. They were the girls of the bawdy houses... the houses of ill fame.

Traverse City, being the lumbering capital of the north, had its share of them. But, let us go on record right now... those young ladies were a part of the community. They were, in most instances, quiet, well-mannered, and pretty.

The lumberjacks who frequented the houses of prostitution are gone, but we recall long visits with many of them and record, for the first time, the really true story of "The Girls" and the part they played in the growing-up of the new middle west.

One thing that seldom comes to the mind of the student of local history is: What happened to the girls who were employed in the local houses of prostitution when they reached an age and were no longer in demand?

Some of them moved on to better or less paying areas. Some of them returned to the big city which spawned them.

But many of them married locally and became homemakers and helpmeets. That is one reason why we are unable to mention names as we recount the little segment of history which meant so much to every boisterous and growing community. There are grandchildren and great grandchildren of some of the girls who were employed in the houses of prostitution in Traverse City. And they live right in the Grand Traverse Bay Region.

Early in the days of Traverse City, there was no merchandising of sex. Any contract was an occasional one of personal culmination. There was no place of organized assignation.

One of the first houses of prostitution in Traverse City was known as the Swamp House. It was a frame house on the east side of Franke road just off Silver Lake road. The girls were known among the lumberjacks as the "Swamp Angels" and were held in considerable esteem.

Most famous of the bordellos was one operated by one Mrs. Moore. It was already established when she arrived from Grand Rapids to take over the going business. She purchased the interest in the establishment which was located near the intersection of Peninsula drive and East Front street.

Despite the fact that most of the girls were "second string," there was always a booming business when the boys were in town.

The former owners of the place purchased by Mrs. Moore were divorced and each established similar business enterprises within the city. One of these houses of prostitution was located where Pine Grove Trailer Park is now situated on Munson Avenue.

Most of the places operated within and near the city and were of good reputation . . . among their constituants. In fact, the owner of a theater in Traverse City would, on occasion, stop by one of them to play a banjo and lend a little life to the parties.

Mrs. Moore offered a rate of $3.00 for an appointment or $5.00 for all night.

Following the sale of the Front street institution to Mrs. Moore, the other partner opened a bumboat on Grand

Traverse Bay and, according to word-of-mouth reports, employed five girls. The boat operated part of one season and sank just off Brosch street, now Eastern Avenue. The old hull is, according to reports, still in deep water at that location.

One of the better known houses was located about three miles out the present M-22 in Leelanau County. To reach such scattered places, Jay Hillicker operated a breech loading hack. He ran into an early problem with his "pay as you leave" system. One by one, the boys would drop off on the return trip and Jay would arrive back at his downtown stand minus a pay load. Shortly he converted to a "pay as you enter" system.

In later years there was a well known bordello located on Mitchell creek, south of the airport. The cabin, called "Mammy's," operated with from four to six girls. Despite the fact that Mammy was black, she hired white girls from the Grand Rapids area.

Mammy was well respected and made no effort to deny her trade. She openly invited local businessmen and other residents to take advantage of special rates for holiday seasons. Her fee was five dollars.

During the depression days, a group of Traverse City do-gooders, working under the guise of Klansmen, dynamited Mammy's house. All that remained standing was one wall on which hung a Christus.

Later Mammy opened a place on Barlow street and, still later, moved to Woodmere.

But society frowned. Business waned. Mammy closed her doors.

The day of the small town bordello was gone. The only monument to their memory is the occasional comment by one of the passing generation. Not many of the menfolk care to comment and the womenfolk are innocent of knowledge ... in most instances.

However, there was an era of promiscuity in Traverse City about which everyone knew. It was those depression days when Puggity-boo and Dollar Bill were practicing their art without a semblance of headquarters or the direction of a "madam."

From whence they came, no one seemed to know. The only fact, known to all and sundry, was that each was a "woman of the streets" and that Puggity-boo hated Dollar Bill with a passion and the hate was reciprocal.

Each had a sort of district in the city of Traverse City and each kept pretty much within its boundaries. Dollar Bill frequented the railroads yards where Clinch Park and the municipal parking area are now located. Puggity-boo wandered the area to the south and east side of the city and the railroad yards on the shore of Boardman lake.

Invasion of territory was a crass insult. Neighbors on Webster street called police one late afternoon and reported that the two mortal enemies were having a friendly stone-throwing contest in the 900 block. It seems that Dollar Bill had gone too far afield and had been challenged.

Of the two, Dollar Bill was the most devoted to intoxicants. If it would pour, Dollar Bill would try it. On one occassion she was arrested in a wooded, vacant lot. She was in low gear from drinking industrial alcohol. Officers picked up seven empty bottles when they arrested her.

While simple charges were placed against the two ladies of the night, action was seldom taken by the authorities. Dollar Bill had the longest arrest record, probably because her field of operation was closer to the downtown area.

Following the closing of the last of the recognized bordellos in Traverse City, there was, once again, a new era of self-sale. With the closing of Mammy's place, several girls with winsom way and willowy waist found themselves out of work... the only work they knew.

As a result of this situation, they took individual rooms in various parts of the city and plied their ancient trade. Of these young ladies, a few remained in the community and eventually married well.

Another segment of the group simply retired from the scene, removing to other and more populated communities.

This phase of the colorful era remained until a short time after the 18th amendment was repealed and beverages became legalized. The wane of bootleg booze took from the ladies-of-the-night one of their sources of income. Most of them knew they could buy a pint, a quart, or a gallon; possibly of questionable quality, but all was intoxicating.

Two young ladies in particular had an "in" with a local purveyor of illegal beverage. The first step in a dating routine was not a dine and dance affair. It was a trip to an east side home where bootleg alcohol was served from a tea kettle, always kept ready on the kitchen cabinet or on the back of an old wood-burning stove.

On occasions, one lady commented, her weekly take from the sale of bootleg was more than her other income. That is a lot of beverage because the going price for a drink was 25c... sometimes as much as 35c in the more posh places.

So it is, the girls who "came down from Buffalo a-drinking ale and wine" are gone. Even the memories faded with the death of the last true lumberjack who was witness to the transition of which the ladies-of-the-evening were a part.

RED MEN'S REBUKE
by
Simon Pokagon
* * *

About Simon Pokagon

Simon Pokagon was the last chief of the Pokagon band of Pottawattamie Indians in southern Michigan. He was born in 1830 at the Pottawattamie village about a mile from the St. Joseph river in St. Joseph county, Michigan. He died in 1899 in Allegan county, Michigan.

Chief Simon Pokagon attended Notre Dame, Oberlin College, and Twinsburg (Ohio) College. He spoke several languages and was a prolific writer. His articles and poetry were widely published.

In 1893, the great Columbian Exposition was being held in Chicago and Chief Pokagon was requested to, with his people, participate. His response to the invitation was "Red Men's Rebuke" which he wrote and published on white birch bark. There is no record of how many copies of the Rebuke were printed, but one of the few existing originals is available for inspection at the Pioneer Study building at the Pathfinder School in Traverse City.

Al Barnes
Ma-Ing-Gan
(Timber Wolf)

Named by the Northern Michigan Ottawa Association on June 10, 1964. Robert Dominic, president.

My object in publishing "Red Men's Rebuke" on the bark of the white birch tree is out of loyalty to my own people, in gratitude to the Great Spirit who, in His great wisdom provided it for our use. For untold generations this remarkable tree with manifold bark, was used by our people instead of paper; being of great value to us as it could not be injured by sun or water.

Out of the bark of this wonderful tree were made hats, caps, and dishes for domestic use, while our maidens tied it the knot which sealed their marriage vows. Wigwams were made of it, as well as large canoes that outrode the violent storms on lake and sea. It was also used for light and fuel at our war councils and spirit dances. Originally the shores of our northern lakes and streams were fringed with it and were evergreen, and the white charmingly contrasted with the green mirrored from the water was, indeed, beautiful. But, like the Red Man, this tree is vanishing from our forests.

* * *

"Shall not one line lament our forest race,
For you struck from wild creation's face?
Freedom—the selfsame freedom you adore,
Bade us defend our violated shore."

* * *

In behalf of my people, the American Indians, I hereby declare to you, the pale-faced race that has usurped our lands, and homes, that we have no spirit to celebrate with you tne Columbian Fair now being held in the Chicago city, the wonder of the world.

No; sooner would we hold high joy-day over the graves of our departed fathers, than to celebrate our own funeral, the discovery of America. And while you who are strangers, and you live here, bring the offerings of the handiwork of your own lands, and your hearts in admiration, rejoice over the beauty and the grandeur of this young republic, and you say, "Behold the wonders wrought by our children in this foreign land," do not forget that this success has been at the sacrifice of our homes and a once happy race.

Where these great Columbian show-buildings stretch skyward, and where stand this "Queen City of the West," once stood the red man's wigwam; here met their old men, young men, and maidens; here blazed their councilfires. But now the eagle's eye can find no trace of them. Here was the center of their wide-spread hunting-grounds; stretching far eastward, and to the great salt Gulf southward, and to the lofty Rocky Mountain chain westward; and all about and beyond the Great Lakes northward roamed vast herds of buffalo that no man could number, while moose, deer and elk were found from ocean to ocean; pigeons, ducks, and geese in near bow-shot moved in great clouds through the air, while fish swarmed our streams, lakes, and seas close to shore. All were provided by the Great Spirit for our use; we destroyed none except for food and dress; had plenty and were contented and happy.

But alas! the pale-faces came by chance to our shores, many times very needy and hungry. We nursed and fed them—fed the ravens that were soon to pluck out our eyes, and the eyes of our children; for no sooner had the news reached the Old World that a new continent had been found, peopled with another race of man, then, locust-like, they swarmed on all our coasts; and, like the carrion crows in spring, that in circles wheel and clamor long and loud, and will not cease until they find and feast upon the dead, so these strangers from the East long circuits made, and turkey-like they gobbled in our ears, "Give us gold, give us gold." "Where find you gold? Where find you gold?"

We gave for promises and "gewgaws" all the gold we had, and showed them where to dig for more; to repay us, they robbed our homes of fathers, mother, sons, and daughters; some were forced across the sea for slaves in Spain, while multitudes were dragged in the mines to dig for gold, and held in slavery there until all who escaped not, died under the lash of the cruel task-master. It finally passed into their history that, "the red man of the West, unlike the black man of the East, will die before he'll be a slave." Our hearts were crushed by such base ingratitude;

and, as the United States has now decreed, "No Chinaman shall land upon our shores," so we then felt that no such barbarians as they, should land on ours.

In those days that tried our fathers' souls, tradition says: "A crippled, grey-haired sire told his tribe that in the vision of the night he was lifted high above the earth, and in great wonder beheld a vast spider-web spread out over the land from the Atlantic Ocean toward the setting sun. Its network was made of rods of iron; along its lines in all directions rushed monstrous spiders, greater in strength, and larger far than any beast of earth, clad in brass and iron, dragging after them long rows of wigwams with families therein, outstripping in their course the flight of birds that fled before them. Hissing from their nostrils came forth fire and smoke, striking terror to both fowl and beast. The red men hid themselves in fear, or fled away, while the white man trained these monsters for the war path, as warriors for battle."

The old man who saw the vision claimed that it meant that the Indian race would surely pass away before the pale-faced strangers. He died a martyr to his belief. Centuries have passed since that time, and we now behold in the vision as in a mirror, the present net-work of railroads, and the monstrous engines with their fire, smoke, and hissing steam, with cars attached, as they go sweeping through the land.

The cyclone of civilation rolled westward; the forests of untold centuries were swept away; streams dried up; lakes fell back from their ancient bounds; and all our fathers once loved to gaze upon was destroyed, defaced, or marred, except the sun, moon and starry skies above, which the Great Spirit in his wisdom hung beyond their reach.

Still on the storm-cloud rolled, while before its lightning and thunder the beasts of the field and the fowls of the air withered like grass before the flame—were shot for love of power to kill alone, and left to spoil upon the plains. Their bleaching bones now scattered far and near, in shame declare the wanton cruelty of pale-faced men. The storm unsatisfied on land swept our lakes and streams, while before its clouds of hooks, nets, and glistening spears the fish vanished from our waters like the morning dew before the rising sun. Thus our inheritance was cut off, and we were driven and scattered as sheep before the wolves.

Nor was this all. They brought among us fatal diseases our fathers knew not of; our medicine-men tried in vain to check the deadly plague; but they themselves died, and our people fell as fall the leaves before the autumn's blast. To be just, we must acknowledge there were some good men with these strangers, who gave their lives for ours, and in great kindness taught us the revealed will of the Great Spirit through his son, Jesus, the meditator between God and man. But while we were being taught to love the Lord our God with all our heart, mind and strength, and our neighbors as ourselves, and our children were taught to lisp, "Our Father who art in heaven, hallowed be thy name," bad men of the same race, whom we thought of the same belief, shocked our faith in the revealed will of the Father, as they came among us with bitter oaths upon their lips, something we had never heard before, and cups of "fire-water" in their hands, something we had never seen before. They pressed the sparkling glasses to our lips and said, "Drink, and you will be happy." We drank thereof, we and our children, but alas! like the serpent that charms to kill, the drink-habit coiled about the heart-strings of its victims, shocking unto death, friendship, love, honor, manhood—all that makes men good and noble; crushing out all ambition, and leaving naught but a culprit vagabond in the place of a man.

Now as we have been taught to believe that our first parents ate of the forbidden fruit, and fell, so we as fully believe that this fire-water is the hard cider of the white man's devil, made from the fruit of that tree that brought death into the world, and all our woes. The arrow, the scalping-knife, and the tomahawk used on the war-path were merciful compared with it; they were used in our defense, but the accursed drink came like a serpent in the form of a dove. Many of our people partook of it without mistrust, as children pluck the flowers and clutch a scorpion in their grasp; only when they feel the sting, they let the flower fall. But Nature's children had no such power; for when the viper's fangs they felt, they only hugged the reptile the more closely to their breasts, while friends before them stood pleading with prayers and tears that they would let the deadly serpent drop. But all in vain. Although they promised so to do, yet with laughing grin and steps uncertain like the fool, they still more frequently guzzled down this hellish drug. Finally, conscience ceased to give alarm, and, led by deep despair to life's last brink, and goaded by demons on every side, they cursed themselves, they cursed their friends, they cursed their beggar babes and wives, they cursed their God, and died.

You say of us that we are treacherous, vindictive and cruel; in answer to the charge, we declare to all the world with our hands uplifted before high Heaven, that before the white man came among us, we were kind, outspoken, and forgiving. Our real character has been misunderstood because we have resented the breaking of the treaties made with the United States, as we honestly understood them. The few of our children who are permitted to attend your schools, in great pride tell us that they read in your own histories, how William Penn, a Quaker, and a good man, made treaties with ninteen tribes of Indians, and that neither he nor they ever broke them; and further, that during seventy years, while Pennsylvania was controlled by the Quakers, not a drop of blood was shed nor a war-whoop sounded by our people. Your own historians, and our traditions, show that for nearly two hundred years, different Eastern powers were striving for the mastery in the new world, and that our people were persuaded by the different factions to take war-path, being generally led by white men who had been discharged from prisons for crimes committed in the Old World.

Read the following, left on record by Peter Martyr, who visited our forefathers in the day of Columbus.

"It is certain that the land among these people is as common as the sun and water, and that mine and thine, the seed of all misery, have no place with them. They are not content with so little, that in so large a country they have rather a superfluity rather than a scarceness: so that they seem to live in the golden world without toil, living in open gardens not intrenched with dykes, divided with hedges, or defended with walls. They deal truly, one with another, without laws, without books, without judges. They take him for an evil mischevious man, who taketh pleasure in doing hurt to another, and albeit they delight not in superfluities, yet they make provision for the increase of such roots whereof they make bread, content with such simple diet whereof health is preserved, and disease avoided."

Your own histories show that Columbus on his first visit to our shores, in a message to the king and queen of Spain, paid our forefathers this beautiful tribute:-

"They are loving uncovetous people: so docile in all things that I swear to you your majesties there is not in the world a better race or a more delightful country. They love their neighbors as themselves, and their talk is ever sweet and gentle, accompanied with smiles; and though they be naked, yet their manners are decorous and praise-worthy."

But a few years passed away, and your historians left to be perused with shame, the following facts:—

"On the islands of the Atlantic coast and in the populous empires of Mexico and Peru, the Spainiards, through pretense of friendship and religion, gained audience with chiefs and kings, their families and attendants. They were received with great kindness and courtesy, but in return they most treacherously seized and bound in chains the unsuspecting natives; and as a ransom for their release, demanded large sums of gold which were soon given by their subjects. But instead of granting them freedom as promised, they were put to death in a most shocking manner. Their subjects were then hunted down by wild beasts, with bloodhounds, robbed and enslaved; while under pretext to convert them to Christianity, the rack, the scourge, and the fagot were used. Some were burned alive in their thickets and fastnesses for refusing to work the mines as slaves."

Tradition says these acts of base ingratitude were

communicated from tribe to tribe throughout the continent, and that a universal wail as one voice went up from all the tribes of the unbroken wilderness: "We must beat back these strangers from our shores before they seize our lands and homes, or slavery and death are ours."

Reader, pause here, close your eyes, shut out from your heart all prejudice against our race, and honestly consider the above records penned by the pale-faced historians centuries ago; and tell us in the name of eternal truth, and by all that is sacred and dear to mankind, was there ever a people without the slightest reason of offense, more treacherously imprisoned and scourged than we have been? And tell us, have crime, despotism, violence, and slavery ever been dealt out in a more wicked manner than to crush out life and liberty; or was ever a people more mortally offended than our forefathers were?

Almighty Spirit of humanity, let thy arms of compassion embrace and shield us from the charge of treachery, vindictiveness, and cruelty, and save us from further oppression! And may the chief of the United States appoint no more broken down or disappointed politicians as agents to deal with us, but may we select good men that are tried and true, men who fear not to do the right. This is our prayer. What would remain for us if we were not allowed to pray? All else we acknowledge to be in the hands of this great republic.

It is clear that for years after the discovery of this country, we stood before the coming strangers, as a block of marble before the sculptor, ready to be shaped into a statue of grace and beauty; but in their greed for gold, the block was hacked to pieces and destroyed. Child-like we trusted in them with all our hearts; and as the young nestling while yet-blind, swallows each morsel given by the parent bird, so we drank in all they said. They showed us the compass that guided them across the trackless deep, and as its needle swung to and fro only resting to the north, we looked upon it as a thing of life from only the eternal world. We could not understand the lightning and thunder of their guns, believing they were weapons of the gods; nor could we fathom thier wisdom in knowing and telling us the exact time in which the sun and moon should be darkened; hence we looked upon them as divine; we revered them—yes, we trusted in them, as infants trust in the arms of their mothers.

But again and again was our confidence betrayed, until we were compelled to know that greed for gold was all the balance-wheel they had. The remnant of the beasts are now wild and keep beyond the arrow's reach, the fowls fly high in the air, the fish hide themselves in deep waters. We have been driven from the homes of our childhood and from the burial places of our kindred and friends, and scattered far westward into desert places, where multitudes have died from homesickness, cold, hunger, and are suffering and dying ill for want of food and blankets.

As the hunted deer close chased all day long, when night comes on, weary and tired, lies down to rest, mourning for companions of the morning herd, all scattered, dead, and gone, so we through weary years have tried to find some place to safely rest. But all in vain! Our throbbing hearts unceasing say, "The hounds are howling on our tracks." Our sad history has been told by weeping parents to their children from generation to generation; and as the fear of the fox in the duckling is hatched, so the wrongs we have suffered are transmitted to our children, and they look upon the white man with distrust as soon as they are born. Hence our worst acts of cruelty should be viewed by all the world with Christian charity, as being but the echo of bad treatment dealt out to us.

Therefore we pray our critics everywhere to be not like the thoughtless boy who condemns the toiling bees wherever found, as vindictive and cruel, because in robbing their homes he once received the poisoned darts that nature gave for their defense. Our strongest defense against the onward marching hordes, we fully realize is as useless as the struggles of a lamb borne high in the air, pierced to its heart, in the talons of an eagle.

We never shall be happy here anymore; we gaze into the faces of our little ones, for smiles of infancy to please, and into the faces of our young men and maidens, for joys of youth to cheer advancing age, but alas! instead of smiles of joy we find but looks of sadness there. Then we fully realize in the anguish of our souls that their young and tender hearts, in keenest sympathy with ours, have drank in the sorrows we have felt, and their sad faces reflect it back to us again. No rainbow of promise spans the dark cloud of our afflictions; no cheering hopes are painted on our midnight sky. We only stand with folded arms and watch and wait to see the future deal with us no better than the past. No cheer of sympathy is given us; but in answer to our complaints we are told the triumphal march of the Eastern race westward is by the unalterable decree of nature, termed by them "the survival of the fittest." And so we stand as upon the seashore, chained hand and foot, while the incoming tide of the great ocean of civilization rises slowly but surely to overwhelm us.

But a few more generations and the last child of the forest will have passed into the world beyond—into that kingdom where Tche-ban-you-booz, the Great Spirit, dwelleth, who loveth justice and mercy, and hateth evil; who has declared the "fittest" in his kingdom shall be those alone who hear and aid his children when they cry, and that love him and keep his commandments. In that kingdom many of our people in faith believe he will summon the pale-faced spirits to take position on his left, and the red spirits on his right, and that he will say, "Sons and daughters of the forest, your prayers for deliverence from the iron heel of oppression through centuries past are recorded in this book now open before me, made from the bark of the white birch, a tree under which for generations past you have mourned and wept. On its pages silently has been recorded your sad history. It has touched my heart with pity and I will have compassion."

Then turning to his left he will say, "Sons and daughters of the East, all hear and give heed unto my words. While on earth I did great and marvelous things for you—I gave my only Son, who declared unto you my will, and as you had freely received, to so freely give, and declare the gospel unto all people. A few of you have kept the faith; and through opposition and great tribulation have labored hard and honestly for the redemption of mankind regardless of race or color. To all such I now give divine power to fly on lightning wings throughout my universe. Now, therefore, listen; and when the great drum beats, let all try their powers to fly. Only those can rise who acted well their part on earth to redeem and save the fallen."

The drum will be sounded, and that innumerable multitude will appear like some vast sea of wounded birds struggling to rise. We shall hear their fluttering as the rumbling of an earthquake, and to our surprise shall see but a scattering few in triumph rise, and hear their songs re-echo through the vault of heaven as they sing, "Glory, to the highest who hath redeemed and saved us."

Then the great Spirit will speak with a voice of thunder to the remaining shame-faced multitude: "Hear ye: it is through great mercy that you have been permitted to enter these happy hunting grounds. Therefore I charge you in presence of these red men that you are gulity of having tyrannized over them in many and strange ways. I find you gulity of having made wanton wholesale butchery of their game and fish, I find you guilty of using tobacco, a poisonous weed made only to kill parasites on plants and lice on man and beast. You found it with the red men, who used it only in smoking the pipe of peace, to confirm their contracts, in place of a seal. But you multiplied its use, not only in smoking, but in chewing, snuffing, thus forming unhealthy, filthy habits, and by cigarettes, the abominations of abominations, learned little children to hunger and thirst after the father and mother of palsy and cancers.

"I find you guilty of tagging after the pay agents sent out by the great chief of the United States, among the Indians, to pay off their birth-right claims to home, and liberty, and native lands, and then sneaking about their agencies by deceit and trickery, cheating and robbing them of their money and goods, thus leaving them poor and naked. I also find you guilty of following the trail of Christian missionaries into the wilderness among the natives, and when they had set up my altars, and the great work of redemption had just begun, and some in faith believed, you then and there most wickedly set up the idol of man-tchi-man-in-to (the devil), and there stuck out your sign, SAMPLE ROOMS. You then dealt out to the sons of the forest a most damnable drug, fitly termed on earth by Christian women, 'a beverage of hell,' which destroyed both body and soul, taking therefore, all their money and blankets, and scrupling not to take in pawn the Bibles given them by my servants.

"Therefore know ye, this much-abused race shall enjoy the liberties of these happy hunting-grounds, while I teach them my will, which you were in duty bound to do while on earth. But instead you blocked up the highway that led to heaven, that the car of salvation might not pass over. Had you done your duty, they as well as you would now be rejoicing in glory with my saints with whom you, fluttering, tried this day in vain to rise. But now I say unto you, Stand back! you shall not tread upon the heels of my people, nor tyrannize over them anymore. Neither shall you with gatling-gun or otherwise disturb or break up their prayer-meetings in camp anymore. Neither shall you practice with weapons of lightning and thunder anymore. Neither shall you use tobacco in any shape, way, or manner. Neither shall you touch, taste, handle, make, buy, or sell anything that can intoxicate anymore. And know ye, ye cannot buy the law or skulk by justice here; and if any attempt is made on your part to break these commandments, I shall forthwith grant these red men of America great power, and delegate them to cast you out of paradise, and hurl you headlong through its outer gates into the endless abyss beneath—far beyond, where darkness meets with light, there to dwell, and thus shut you out from my presence and the presence of angels and the light of heaven forever and ever."